Rigor and Asse in the Classr

Learn how to assess students in a way that truly impacts learning. In *Rigor and Assessment in the Classroom,* bestselling author Barbara R. Blackburn provides a broad range of practical strategies for increasing the rigor and usefulness of your formative and summative assessments. You'll discover how to . . .

- Create an environment where students are expected to learn at high levels;
- Evaluate and check student learning in a way that ensures growth;
- Strengthen the validity and reliability of your assessments;
- Plan assessments in conjunction with planning the instruction;
- Differentiate assessments to increase the rigor for all students;
- Enhance the effectiveness of your grading system and feedback;
- Use performance-based assessment to enhance rigor; and
- Design clear, reader-friendly rubrics and scoring guides.

Each chapter includes ready-to-use tools, examples across the subject areas, and "Think About It" questions to help you reflect on what you've read. Many of the tools are also offered as free eResources at www.routledge.com/9781138936140, so you can easily print and distribute them for classroom use.

Dr. Barbara R. Blackburn is the bestselling author of sixteen books and is a sought-after consultant (www.barbarablackburnonline.com). She was an award-winning professor at Winthrop University and has taught students of all ages.

Rigor and Assessment in the Classroom

Barbara R. Blackburn

 Routledge
Taylor & Francis Group

NEW YORK AND LONDON

KH

First published 2017
by Routledge
711 Third Avenue, New York, NY 10017

and by Routledge
2 Park Square, Milton Park, Abingdon, Oxon, OX14 4RN

Routledge is an imprint of the Taylor & Francis Group, an informa business

Library of Congress Cataloging in Publication Data
A catalog record has been requested.

ISBN: 978-1-138-93613-3 (hbk)
ISBN: 978-1-138-93614-0 (pbk)
ISBN: 978-1-315-67702-6 (ebk)

Typeset in Palatino
by Florence Production Ltd, Stoodleigh, Devon, UK

10/18/17

Dedication

To my stepfather-in-law, Gene, whose wisdom
provides a legacy to his family.

Contents

WITHDRAWN

Meet the Author

Dr. Barbara Blackburn has dedicated her life to raising the level of rigor and motivation for professional educators and students alike. What differentiates Barbara's sixteen books are her easily executable concrete examples based on decades of experience as a teacher, professor, and consultant. Barbara's dedication to education was inspired in her early years by her parents. Her father's doctorate and lifetime career as a professor taught her the importance of professional training. Her mother's career as a school secretary shaped Barbara's appreciation of the effort all staff play in the education of every child. Barbara has taught early childhood, elementary, middle, and high school students, and has served as an educational consultant for three publishing companies. She holds a master's degree in school administration and was certified as a teacher and principal in North Carolina. She received her Ph.D. in Curriculum and Teaching from the University of North Carolina at Greensboro. In 2006, she received the award for Outstanding Junior Professor at Winthrop University. She left her position at the University of North Carolina at Charlotte to write and speak full-time.

In addition to speaking at state and national conferences, she also regularly presents workshops for teachers and administrators in elementary, middle, and high schools. Her workshops are lively and engaging and filled with practical information. Her most popular topics include:

- Rigor is NOT a Four-Letter Word
- Rigorous Schools and Classrooms: Leading the Way
- Motivation + Engagement + Rigor = Student Success
- Rigor for Students with Special Needs
- Instructional Strategies that Motivate Students
- Content Literacy Strategies for the Young and the Restless
- Motivating Yourself and Others
- Engaging Instruction Leads to Higher Achievement
- High Expectations and Increased Support Lead to Success

Barbara can be reached through her website: www.barbarablackburnonline.com.

Acknowledgments

To my husband, Pete. Your love and encouragement is essential to my work.

A special thank you to my dad, who reads and reflects on everything I write.

Thank you to my family—Mom, Becky, Brenda, and Hunter for your continuing support.

To Abbigail Armstrong, thank you for all your help with practical examples throughout the book.

To Lauren Davis, my editor, you have a gift for knowing how to take my ideas and helping me communicate them effectively.

To Jessica Bennett, Susan Gorman, Karen Hickman, and Nikki Mouton—thanks for your suggestions, which helped me clarify and refine the content.

To Kamae Design, thank you for a wonderful cover design.

To Claire Handy and Florence Production, thanks for the great jobs you did in copyediting and page make-up.

Finally, to the teachers and leaders in my workshops and all those who read my books and use the ideas to impact students, thank you. You make a difference every day in the lives of your students.

eResources

As you read this book, you'll notice the eResources icon next to the following tools. The icon indicates that these tools are available as free downloads on our website, www.routledge.com/9781138936140, so you can easily print and distribute them to your students.

Introduction

Rigor and Assessment in the Classroom developed out of the questions and requests from teachers and leaders in my workshops. Many had read my earlier books on rigor: *Rigor is NOT a Four-Letter Word, Rigor Made Easy, Rigor for Students with Special Needs, Rigor Made Easy,* and *Rigor in Your Classroom: A Toolkit for Teachers.* Each of those focused on a variety of strategies to use in the classroom to increase rigor, and they included sections on assessment.

However, participants wanted more, specifically on assessment. Assessment is such a challenging issue in today's classrooms. How do we assess students in a way that impacts learning? How do we ensure rigor in those assessments? Based on these questions, I wrote this book.

Throughout the book, I focus on the various types of rigorous assessments you can use in your class to make a difference with your students. We'll look at best practices in rigor and assessment, how to plan assessments, and how instruction and assessment interrelate. Then, we'll turn to formative assessments, summative assessments, performance-based assessments, differentiated assessments, grading, and feedback. In the final chapter, we'll discuss how you can work with other teachers to improve your assessments.

Although I'd recommend you start with Chapter 1, the rest of the chapters can be read in any order—start with the one you are most interested in. Also, as you read about the variety of strategies, don't try to implement everything at one time. If you do, it will be overwhelming. Rather, try one or two ideas and see how they work. Take time to implement them and adjust as needed. Then, try something else.

As a final note, I chose not to address standardized testing in this book. The focus is on assessment you can use on a regular basis in your classroom. That doesn't mean standardized testing isn't an important part of your class, but you typically don't have control over it. And I believe in helping teachers improve instruction through things they can control.

I hope you enjoy the book and find the ideas to be practical. I've also included reflection activities, for yourself, or to be used in a book study. If you'd like to give me feedback, or ask about professional development, please contact me through my website, www.barbarablackburnonline.com, or via Twitter @barbblackburn.

1

Best Practices in Rigor and Assessment

Rigor

Instructional rigor is a key component of effective instruction. Too often, we think that our instruction is rigorous, but it is not. Our assumptions about rigor, as well as our practices, make a difference in what we expect from students. In this chapter, we'll explore the myths of rigor, turn our attention to what best practice in instructional rigor is, then look at similar best practices in assessment.

Defining Rigor

Despite all the research, there are seven commonly held myths about rigor.

Seven Myths

- Lots of homework is a sign of rigor.
- Rigor means doing more.
- Rigor is not for everyone.
- Providing support means lessening rigor.
- Resources equal rigor.
- Standards alone take care of rigor.
- Rigor is just one more thing to do.

Now that we have looked at what rigor is *not*, let's look at what rigor *is*. In *Rigor is Not a Four-Letter Word*, I define rigor as "creating an environment in which . . .

- each student is expected to learn at high levels;
- each student is supported so he or she can learn at high levels; and
- each student demonstrates learning at high levels."

Notice we are looking at the environment you create. The tri-fold approach to rigor is not limited to the curriculum that students are expected to learn. It is more than a specific lesson or instructional strategy. It is deeper than what a student says or does in response to a lesson. True rigor is the result of weaving together all elements of schooling to raise students to higher levels of learning. Let's take a deeper look at the three aspects of the definition.

Expecting Students to Learn at High Levels

The first component of rigor is creating an environment in which each student is expected to learn at high levels. Having high expectations starts with the recognition that every student possesses the potential to succeed at his or her individual level.

Almost every teacher or leader I talk with says, "We have high expectations for our students." Sometimes that is evidenced by the behaviors in the school; other times, however, faculty actions don't match the words. There are concrete ways to implement and assess rigor in classrooms.

As you design lessons that incorporate more rigorous opportunities for learning, you will want to consider the questions that are embedded in the instruction. Higher-level questioning is an integral part of a rigorous classroom. Look for open-ended questions, ones that are at the higher levels of Bloom's Taxonomy (analysis, synthesis).

It is also important to pay attention to how you respond to student questions. When we visit schools, it is not uncommon to see teachers who ask higher-level questions. But for whatever reason, we then see some of the same teachers accept low-level responses from students. In rigorous classrooms, teachers push students to respond at high levels. They ask extending questions. Extending questions are questions that encourage students to explain their reasoning and think through ideas. When a student does not know the immediate answer but has sufficient background information to provide a response to the question, the teacher continues to probe and guide the student's thinking rather than moving on to the next student. Insist on thinking and problem solving.

Supporting Students to Learn at High Levels

High expectations are important, but the most rigorous schools assure that each student is supported so he or she can learn at high levels, which is the second part of our definition. It is essential that teachers design lessons that move students to more challenging work while simultaneously providing ongoing scaffolding to support students' learning as they move to those higher levels.

Providing additional scaffolding throughout lessons is one of the most important ways to support your students. Oftentimes students have the ability or knowledge to accomplish a task but are overwhelmed by the complexity of it, therefore getting lost in the process. This can occur in a variety of ways, but it requires that teachers ask themselves during every step of their lessons, "What extra support might my students need?"

Examples of Scaffolding Strategies

- Asking guiding questions
- Chunking information
- Highlighting or color-coding steps in a project
- Writing standards as questions for students to answer
- Using visuals and graphic organizers such as a math graphic organizer for word problems, maps to accompany history lessons, or color-coded paragraphs to help students make meaning of texts

---

Ensuring Students Demonstrate Learning at High Levels

The third component of a rigorous classroom is providing each student with opportunities to demonstrate learning at high levels. A teacher recently said to us, "If we provide more challenging lessons that include extra support, then learning will happen." What we've learned is that if we want students to show us they understand what they learned at a high level, we also need to provide opportunities for students to demonstrate they have truly mastered that learning. In order for students to demonstrate their learning, they must first be engaged in academic tasks, precisely those in the classroom.

Student engagement is a critical aspect of rigor. In too many classrooms, most of the instruction consists of the teacher-centered, large-group instruction, perhaps in an interactive lecture or discussion format. The general practice during these lessons is for the teacher to ask a question and then call on a student to respond. While this provides an opportunity for one student to demonstrate understanding, the remaining students don't do so.

Another option would be for the teacher to allow all students to pair-share, respond with thumbs up or down, write their answers on small whiteboards and share their responses, or respond on handheld computers that tally the responses. Such activities hold each student accountable for demonstrating his or her understanding.

THINK ABOUT IT!

How do you incorporate rigor in your classroom?

Assessment

In addition to rigor, assessment is a key part of the learning process. Almost every researcher on assessment has developed criteria for effective assessment. Although there are some differences between individual researchers, generally, there are seven key principles.

---

7 Principles of Effective Assessment

1. Informs and transforms
2. Comprehensive
3. Aligned
4. Developmentally appropriate
5. Quality
6. Involves students
7. Results are effectively communicated

Informs and Transforms

Effective assessment informs both the teacher and the student, but it also transforms the teaching and learning experience. Assessment provides information to the teacher about what students know and do not know, which allows him or her to adjust instruction. For example, if all students missed question 12 on a test, but answered all others questions on the same objective correctly, that would lead you to evaluate the question to determine if it was clear to the students. You might reword the question on future tests.

On the other hand, if, in looking at the results of a summative assessment, you discover that 21 of your 28 students missed all questions related to a particular objective, it is likely that your instruction of the objective was not as effective as you thought. Therefore, reteaching is needed.

Assessment should also inform teachers and students about individual strengths and weaknesses. This allows for differentiation of instruction, both in terms of remediation and enrichment. These examples support the notion of transformation, which we'll look at further in Chapter 4.

Truly effective assessment transforms the teaching and learning experience. The information is not simply provided; teachers and students use that information to improve. In the first example given, if the teacher simply says, "Question 12 was a bad question," then so what? But if he or she analyzes what made the question confusing and applies that knowledge to writing future questions, that is transformative.

In the second example, when a teacher actually revisits the content so students can master it, the assessment has transformed the instruction. And in terms of learning about individual strengths and weaknesses, transformation occurs when the student, with the teacher's guidance, improves on weaknesses and builds on strengths to learn at new levels.

Comprehensive

Second, effective assessment is comprehensive. Rather than using assessment as a single snapshot, effective assessment uses multiple types of assessment frequently.

It is important to use different types of assessment because not all students demonstrate learning in the same way. Some students perform well on traditional tests. Others become anxious and can score at a low level, even if they understand the content. Using a variety of measures, including tests, gives you a broader view of what students have learned.

Part of the comprehensive nature of assessment is to use them frequently. When I was teaching, everyone was assessed on Friday. The students called it "test day" because that was all they did. There were two problems with that approach. First, assessment didn't happen at natural times—the tests drove the schedule. Second, one assessment a week wasn't enough to truly know where students were in the learning process.

Robert Marzano in *Classroom Assessment and Grading that Works*, found that frequency was a key measure of student achievement. Although weekly assessment was considered a good minimum, student achievement increased as frequency of assessments increased.

Another reason to use more frequent assessments is to lower the high-stakes measure of a single assessment. I remember my first job at the university. My department chair insisted that all professors have at least four tests or assignments per class. Her perspective was that one assignment or test should not make or break a grade for a student. I agreed. How could one assessment truly measure all that a student learned over a semester?

Aligned

Effective assessment is always aligned with goals, objectives, and instruction. We'll discuss this more in Chapter 2, but let's take a quick look now. This principle may sound like common sense, however, oftentimes assessments are not aligned. They may be a general match to the overall topic, but with an in-depth analysis of the goals and objectives, the mismatch becomes clear.

It's also important to align with your instructional procedures. What do I mean? I observed a teacher during a lesson focused on a series of detailed facts. Much of the lesson was rote learning, and it was clear that students were expected to know the minute details of the information. The next day, students were given a test. Rather than asking students to recall the facts, the essay test required a deep analysis of issues, which included the need to bring in outside information for current applications.

The assessment was rigorous, but it wasn't aligned to the instructional focus and procedures. Based on the lesson, students thought they needed to memorize isolated facts, yet the assessment went much further. We must ensure that we use instructional procedures that match our assessment expectations.

Developmentally Appropriate

Next, effective assessment is developmentally appropriate. Too often, we use measures that are not matched to our students' developmental levels. For example, I was in a first-grade classroom where students were reading about Rosa Parks. The read aloud was appropriate, but the questioning (informal assessment) was not. One of the questions related to the concept of lynching. In this case, although the assignment is rigorous in terms of higher-level questions, it is far too adult for the first graders.

As a part of developmental appropriateness, we must also address authenticity. When assessments seem contrived, they are not as effective. Let's look at this example for middle school students:

Sample Assignment

Solve a set of computational problems related to proportions, geometrical shapes, and rotations.

Notice how the task is not an authentic situation for young adolescents. The rigor and authenticity would be improved if we reframed the assignment.

Quality

Effective assessment is also quality-driven. In the case of assessment, this means that your task, test, project, or other type of assessment is free from errors, is valid, and is reliable.

Free from Errors

Let's begin with the concept of error in assessments. There are two types of errors that can occur. First are systematic errors, which usually occur unintentionally. They can also generally be avoided. Christopher Gareis and Leslie Grant, in *Teacher-Made Assessments: How to Connect Curriculum, Instruction, and Student Learning,* provide examples of systematic error.

Examples of Systematic Error

- Culturally-biased language, idioms, and references
- Developmentally inappropriate reading level
- Mechanical or grammatical mistakes in assessment items
- Insufficient or unclear directions
- Poor layout of the assessment, causing uncertainty or mistakes in reading the assessment
- Insufficient number of assessment items
- Subjective scoring
- Cheating

The second type of error is random error, which is unpredictable. Because of this, it can rarely be controlled. Once again, Gareis and Grant provide examples.

Validity

Validity is another critical aspect of the quality of your assessments. Validity is the appropriateness of the assessment. It answers the question, "Does it assess what it is intended to?" The foundation of validity is the supposition that validity hinges on someone rendering judgments, making decisions, or drawing inferences based on the results of an assessment (Stiggins & Conklin, 1992). In other words, a more accurate definition of validity is the extent to which inferences drawn from assessment results are appropriate (Gareis & Grant, 2015).

If you have an accurate inference about the assessment results, it is valid. If it is an inaccurate inference, then it is not valid.

There are three types of validity. *Construct validity*, or face validity, is when something appears to be valid. Usually, you need content expertise to determine face validity. *Content validity* is how well the assessment matches the instructional objectives and learning outcomes it purports to assess. Finally, *concurrent validity* measures how effectively the assessment matches another assessment that is measuring the same outcomes. The table on the facing page provides questions to guide you as you determine the validity of your assessments.

Reliability

Finally, quality-driven assignments are reliable. Reliability addresses the consistency and stability across assessments. In other words, if you give multiple assessments designed to measure the same objectives or learning outcomes, are the results steady? Are they dependable? They are if your assessment is reliable. Let's turn again to Gareis and Grant for questions to guide your thinking, as well as steps to help ensure reliability.

How to Strengthen the Validity of Teacher-Made Assessments		
Facets of Validity	*Questions a teacher can ask to gauge validity*	*Evidence a teacher can gather to determine and strengthen validity*
Construct Validity	• Can we infer a student's knowledge and skills related to the intended learning outcomes of an instructional unit from the assessment?	• Unpack the intended learning outcomes or objectives that the assessment is intended to tap, and determine their appropriateness for the curricular goals of this unit of instruction (see Chapter 3). • Create a table of specifications and review its adequacy in representing the intended learning outcomes of the instructional unit (see Chapter 3).
Content Validity (a.k.a., *Sampling Validity*)	• Does the assessment adequately sample the intended learning outcomes? • Does the assessment adequately represent the relative importance of the intended learning outcomes?	• Create a table of specifications and review it to ensure that the assessment adequately samples the intended learning outcomes, without over-sampling or under-sampling any intended learning outcomes (see Chapter 3).
Concurrent Validity	• Can we find confirming evidence of learning or predict performance on a related assessment that is designed to measure the same learning objectives?	• Compare performance on another assessment of the intended learning outcomes (e.g., a test created by a colleague, state assessments, Advanced Placement exams.)

Used with permission from Gareis & Grant, 2015.

How to Strengthen the Reliability of a Teacher-Made Assessment	
Questions a teacher can ask to gauge reliability	*Steps a teacher can take to improve reliability*
Do I have *enough questions* for each intended learning outcome that I am assessing?	• As a general rule, include three or more test questions or items for each core objective so as to reduce the unintended effects of error on the assessment results.
Are the *questions, directions, and formatting* on the assessment free from systematic error?	• Review and proofread individual test questions, prompts, and directions for systematic error, including grammatical or mechanical mistakes, cultural biases, and lack of clarity.
Are the *criteria for grading* the assessment as objective as possible?	• Clarify and verify grading criteria for the test, including rubrics. • Ensure *intra-rater* and *inter-rater reliability* by establishing scoring protocols and training.

Used with permission from Gareis & Grant, 2015.

Involves Students

Student involvement is key to effective assessment. If assessments are totally teacher-driven, you won't see the best results. First, assessments should be developed in part based on what you know about your students. If you believe they have already mastered the content, the assessment should reflect that. You would create a project, test, or task in which they have to apply the content to a new situation. If they are still learning the content, you may use a formative assessment to gauge where they are in the learning process. Knowledge of student learning is critical to developing effective assessments.

Students may also be involved by helping create assessments. When I gave tests to my students, one of the ways I reviewed was to have them come up with questions about the content. Then, we discussed the questions and answers. I often used those questions on the test. Many times, they were more rigorous than what I would have created! I also believe students should help develop rubrics for tasks. As you guide them through the development process, they learn the expectations of the assignment. I've heard many students say, "After we built our rubric, I finally knew what I'm supposed to do."

Another way students are involved relates to the informative nature of effective assessments. As I mentioned earlier, the best assessments inform you about learning, and then transform the teaching and learning process. That is part of student involvement. What happens with the student is what provides information to you, so you can take the next instructional steps. If we don't focus on how students perform on assessments, and instead, only focus on the task, we have lost the effectiveness of the assessment.

John Hattie, author of *Visible Learning*, synthesized over 800 meta-studies related to students, teachers, home, curricula, and teaching and learning approaches that impact classroom effectiveness. Based on the studies, he ranked which strategies make the most difference regarding student achievement in terms of effect size. The average size, or hinge point, is .40. The higher the effect size, the more impact there is on student achievement. Self-reporting of grades, another way for students to be involved, is at the top of the list with a 1.44 effect size. It is the most powerful way to positively impact student achievement, and it happens with their involvement.

Results are Effectively Communicated

Finally, with effective assessment, the results are successfully communicated to the teacher, the students, and the parents or families. When you develop an assessment, be sure it will provide you the information you need about student learning. If a test is just a series of questions, will the results communicate to you what students do and do not understand? One way to create tests is to use three levels. Include some questions that are appropriately challenging to the content, then add some basic review questions, and some that are above the level you taught. By looking at which questions students were able to answer, you can better determine if they are still in the review stage, have mastered the content, or have gone beyond the content for new applications.

Results should also be communicated to students in ways they can understand and use. A simple grade on a project usually isn't enough. Whether I achieve an A or a C, how do I know what that means? What did I do well? How could I improve? In this example, it's better to provide specific feedback as to what the grade actually means.

Feedback is one of the most important aspects of assessment. Returning to John Hattie's work on effect sizes, feedback receives a .73, which means it is an effective way to positively impact student learning and achievement. It is so important, I've devoted an entire chapter (Chapter 9) to an in-depth look at how to use comprehensive feedback. For now, know that without appropriate feedback, your assessments lose their adequacy.

Communicating results to parents and family members is also important. The home environment, which is also cited by Hattie as a lower effect size but still a factor in learning, matters. Although we cannot change the environment of the home, we can impact how parents and families respond to and support educational efforts. I've found most parents, regardless of background, want their children to be successful. However, they sometimes don't know how to help and they are sometimes apprehensive of school personnel, many times due to their own bad experiences in school. When we can effectively share what students are doing, how they are learning, and what they still need to know, parents and families can become very supportive. Part of communicating results is also sharing specific strategies with them so they can help. I've met many parents and family members who have told me that they don't know what their child can do, and they don't know how to help him or her become a stronger learner. Sharing this information is part of communicating results, and we'll discuss this more in Chapter 8.

THINK ABOUT IT!

Which of these characteristics of assessment do you need to improve upon in your classroom?

Conclusion

It's important to remember the characteristics of effective rigor and assessment. As we continue our discussion of both, these principles will guide our discussion.

2

Planning for Rigorous Assessments

As we begin our discussion about rigor and assessment, we'll start with planning. You may be wondering why we wouldn't jump into types of rigorous assessments, but the reality is that, without strong planning, you can't have strong assessments. Oftentimes, we use whatever assessment comes with our program—whether that is a textbook or computer resource— add in a few formative assessments, and we think we are done. But the most effective assessment comes from a detailed look at what we want to accomplish, then the development of a plan for accomplishing the goals. For our purposes, we'll look at planning assessments, whether they are formative or summative.

The Planning Process

There are a variety of ways to plan. When I was a first-year teacher, I simply looked through my resources, planned my lesson, and matched it to an objective. Then I wrote or adapted a test or project to measure what my students learned. Now I know that wasn't the best way. However, that process is still used in some classrooms for planning instruction and assessment. But this doesn't necessarily ensure rigor.

An alternative I prefer is the Task Cycle. I researched this model from the DuPont Corporation while working on my doctorate. The Task Cycle focuses on starting with the rationale (or purpose) and desired result (product) before determining the process or resources needed.

Think about how this applies to the classroom. Too often, we start with the process (how to get there) and resources (what we use to teach). For

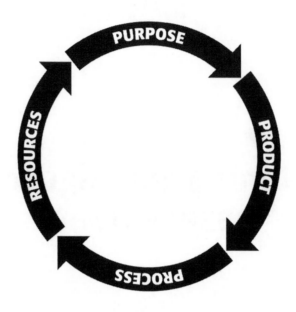

The Task Cycle

example, perhaps what I plan is for students to learn about Martin Luther King, Jr. and the Civil Rights Movement by viewing (process) his "I Have a Dream" speech online (resource).

Let's turn that around with the Task Cycle. The purpose is that we want students to understand the impact Martin Luther King, Jr. had on the Civil Rights Movement (purpose) and we want them to demonstrate their understanding through a podcast (product). To do that, students will need to read about Martin Luther King, Jr. and watch the "I Have a Dream" speech (process) using online news articles and the video (resources).

By starting with our purpose and product, which is the assessment, we can ensure a higher quality, more rigorous lesson. As we move forward in our discussion of the Task Cycle, we will be focusing specifically on assessment. However, the model also applies to instruction, as you saw above.

Purpose

The first part of the Task Cycle is to decide on the purpose. The purpose will be embedded throughout all parts of the cycle. To determine the purpose, we need to clarify some vocabulary. There are several terms that are often used interchangeably, but they actually have different characteristics and areas of focus.

> - Goals
> - Standard
> - Objectives
> - Learning Targets

Goals are broad expectations for students, which can be for multiple grade levels and/or subjects. For example, "students will be lifelong learners" is a typical goal for schools. They may be embedded within our instruction and assessment, but are not necessarily specific to particular strategies and assessments.

Standards are usually content-based, and are limited to a grade level and grade range. Generally, standards are created at the national or state level, and are intended to ensure all students learn the same content during a school year.

Objectives are narrower. Although some may be specific to a lesson, they generally encompass several lessons, perhaps within a unit of instruction. Objectives are designed to guide the teacher when developing instruction and assessment.

Learning Targets differ from objectives in design and purpose. Rather than guiding instruction, they guide learning. As such, they are written from the student's point of view, using student-friendly language. Learning targets are typically written for individual lessons.

Why do these terms matter? In considering them, you may create different assessments for goals and standards than for objectives and learning targets. Understanding them is part of planning for your purpose.

Let's return to the goal of "students becoming lifelong learners." How would you assess that? Perhaps through an anecdotal record of teacher notes related to student behavior that indicates a desire to learn beyond the school day. Or you might have students complete a self-assessment of indicators related to lifelong learning.

On the other hand, standards, objectives, and learning targets will call for different types of assessments. It is likely that standards include many objectives and learning targets. For example, the standard, "Develop an understanding of fractions (i.e., denominators 2, 3, 4, 6, 8, 10) as numbers" includes objectives such as "Students will demonstrate their understanding by representing fractions in various forms such as using a number line." This would translate into the following learning target: "I can represent fractions on a number line."

For our purposes in this chapter, let's look at a sample set of objectives, standards, and learning targets. We'll use these throughout our discussion of the Task Cycle.

Sample Standard

The student will design a map and calculate distances between multiple geographic points.

Corresponding Objectives

- The student will be able to create a sample map using a variety of geographical features.
- The student will be able to create a map scale.
- The student will be able to measure the distance between four geographic points.
- The student will be able to use the map scale to determine the actual distance between the points.

Corresponding Learning Targets

- I can create a sample map with at least four geographical features and a map scale.
- I can measure the distance between the four points in inches and centimeters.
- I can use the map scale to determine the actual distance between the two places.

No matter whether you are planning an assessment for goals, standards, objectives, or learning targets, there are several questions that should guide your planning.

Questions

- Did I match the essential knowledge and skills to the assessment?
- Do students understand what to do and how it relates to the purpose?
- Do I understand how well the students understand the goal, standard, objectives, or learning targets?

Ensuring Rigor in Planning

There are three specific ways to ensure that rigor is incorporated in your planning. First, you must make sure that you start with rigorous goals, standards, objectives, and learning targets. Generally, with the national push for more rigorous standards, we have seen increased challenge and complexity in state and national standards. However, I have seen instances of teachers simplifying those standards into objectives and learning targets, and in the process, watering down the rigor.

How can you ensure that you are truly meeting your standards, etc.? First, look beyond the verbs in the standard. The verb only tells part of the story. A verb such as "apply" can either mean a basic application or an application at a high level, depending on the context of the standard.

Next, measure your objectives and learning targets against a standard measure of rigor. Let's turn to Webb's *Depth of Knowledge* (http://webbalign.org), which we'll discuss in more detail in Chapter 10. Simply take your assignment or assessment and compare it to the levels to determine if it is rigorous, which would be Level Three or above (for example, as shown in the table on the next page).

Finally, we want to ensure that the assessment itself is rigorous. The main strategy for this is to match it to a rigorous goal, standard, objective, or learning target. Then, the design of the assessment must be rigorous.

Product

After you have determined your purpose, then you decide on the product. Since there are a variety of assessments to choose from, you'll want to make sure you plan the best type to match your purpose. Since we'll deal with specific assessments in Chapters 4, 5, and 6, here we'll discuss general principles for choosing or developing a rigorous assessment as your product.

General Principles

- Match the type of assessment to the purpose.
- Incorporate rigor throughout the product.
- Stay on track.

First, match the type of assessment you want to use with the purpose of the assessment. For example, if you want students to demonstrate knowledge of facts, the best assessment may be a multiple-choice question or a short-answer question that requires a list response. But if you want students

Summary Definitions of *Depth of Knowledge* (DOK) for Math			
LEVEL 1	*LEVEL 2*	*LEVEL 3*	*LEVEL 4*
Requires students to recall or observe facts, definitions, and terms. Includes simple one-step procedures. Includes computing simple algorithms (e.g., sum, quotient). *Examples:* • Recall or recognize a fact, term, or property • Represent in words, pictures, or symbols a math object or relationship • Perform a routine procedure, such as measuring • At higher grades, solve a quadratic equation or a system of two linear equations with two unknowns	Requires students to make decisions on how to approach a problem. Requires students to compare, classify, organize, estimate, or order data. Often involves procedures with two or more steps. *Examples:* • Specify and explain relationships between facts, terms, properties, or operations • Select a procedure according to criteria and perform it • Use concepts to solve routine multiple-step problems	Requires reasoning, planning, or use of evidence to solve a problem or algorithm. May involve an activity with more than one possible answer. Requires conjecture or restructuring of problems. Involves drawing conclusions from observations, citing evidence and developing logical arguments for concepts. Uses concepts to solve non-routine problems. *Examples:* • Formulate original problem, given situation • Formulate mathematical model for complex situation • Produce a sound and valid mathematical argument • Devise an original proof • Critique a mathematical argument	Requires complexity at least at the level of DOK 3 but also an extended time to complete the task. A project that requires extended time but repetitive or lower-DOK tasks is not at Level 4. Requires complex reasoning, planning, developing, and thinking. May require students to make several connections and apply one approach among many to solve the problem. May involve complex restructuring of data, establishing and evaluating criteria to solve problems. *Examples:* • Apply a mathematical model to illuminate a problem or situation • Conduct a project that specifies a problem, identifies solution paths, solves the problem, and reports results • Design a mathematical model to inform and solve a practical or abstract situation

Used with permission from WebbAlign © 2016. All Rights Reserved. WebbAlign offers alignment studies and professional development on Webb's *Depth of Knowledge*. Please contact us at contracts@wceps.org or 877-249-4211 for more information.

to demonstrate problem-solving skills as well as an understanding of cross-pollination, a performance-based assessment such as the design and completion of an experiment is more appropriate.

Let's go back to the standards, objectives, and learning targets we detailed in the prior section. For those, there are several pertinent products.

Product(s)

1. Student-designed map with a minimum of four geographical features and a map scale.
2. Labeling of distances between points.
3. Conversion table of actual distances.

Next, incorporate rigor throughout the assessment. As we explore the different types of assessment throughout the book, I'll include specific recommendations for rigor for each type. For now, generally, you should:

- include a focus on higher-order thinking skills;
- include problem-solving;
- include justifications and explanations in responses.

THINK ABOUT IT!

How would you increase the rigor of the products listed?

Finally, be sure you don't get off track. Recently, I was assessing samples of student assignments in elementary, middle, and high schools. One consistent theme I discovered was that many assessments were very creative, but the academic work was not rigorous, nor did they match the goals, standards, objectives, or learning targets. I am a huge believer in creative, engaging activities, but if the assessment is focused on that, you can miss the academic piece. For the samples I evaluated, students spent the majority of their time on the artistic, creative side of the assignment, whether it was creating a flipbook or a Prezi. The assessments provided evidence of students' creativity, but less about their understanding of content. It's particularly important to balance the two.

THINK ABOUT IT!

Look at your latest lesson.
What is the purpose and the product?

Process

In the process part of the cycle, you work backwards from your product. Now that you know where you want to end up, you figure out how to get there. Planning how you teach a lesson is where your creativity can thrive! Think of all the ways you can engage your students, from pair-shares to hands-on activities to technology-based instruction.

Sample Learning Activities

Students are given a variety of maps and asked to identify the geographical features using apps such as Google Earth or Kids World Maps.

With the same maps, use the map scale to measure the distance between various geographical features in inches and centimeters, then convert those numbers to actual distances.

In groups, use MapFab to create a map online. Include a variety of geographical features. Create a map scale and measure the distance between landforms in inches and centimeters, then convert that to actual distances.

Individually, either on paper or online, create a sample map with at least four geographical features and a map scale.

Individually, measure the difference between the four points in inches and centimeters.

Convert the inches and centimeters to the actual distance between places.

You'll want to differentiate the assessment to meet the varying needs of your students. We'll look at differentiation in more depth in Chapter 7, but for now, simply consider your own students' differing needs. Here's sample differentiation activities for the objectives and products in our example.

Sample Differentiation Activities	
Special Needs Students	• Provide a basic outline of a map with four geographical features. • Provide a sample chart of how to convert the distance on a map to actual distance.

Resources

The final part of the Task Cycle to consider is the resources needed. Although you can use the cycle to plan instruction, we will continue to focus on assessment. So, what resources do you need for the assessment itself? If it is a test, you need the test and an answer key. For a performance assessment, you will need the assignment and a rubric. For the products listed in the earlier section, students will need paper, a pencil, a pen, or markers, and a measurement tool.

Another Application

Now that we've discussed the Task Cycle, let's look at how it applies to another standard.

Sample Task Cycle Applied to a Writing Standard	
Purpose	
Standard	• The student will develop a topic sentence and supporting sentences.
Objectives	• The student will be able to identify a topic sentence and supporting sentences in a paragraph. • The student will be able to describe the purpose of a topic sentence and supporting sentences. • The student will be able to evaluate a topic sentence to ensure it represents the paragraph's main idea. • The student will be able to evaluate supporting sentences to ensure they reinforce the paragraph's main idea. • The student will be able to write a paragraph with a topic sentence and supporting sentences.
Learning Goals	• I can identify a topic sentence and supporting sentences. • I can explain the purpose of a topic sentence and supporting sentences. • I can evaluate a topic sentence and describe whether the supporting sentences match the topic sentence. • I can evaluate supporting sentences. • I can write a paragraph with a topic sentence and supporting sentences.

Process
• Using a K-W-L, discuss what students already know about topic sentences and supporting sentences.
• Using a read-aloud or other text selection, lead a discussion about topic and supporting sentences (incorporate pair-shares).
• Play a group matching game of topic and supporting sentences.
• Give small groups of students a text to read. Ask them to create their own matching game of topic and supporting sentences.
• Ask groups to swap cards and texts and play the game. Groups should then justify (either orally or in writing) their responses.

Products
1. Matching and sorting of game cards with topic sentences and supporting details.
2. Short answers to questions of the explanation and purpose of topic sentences and supporting details.
3. Description of whether a topic sentence matches the main idea, after reading a sample text.
4. Written paragraph.

Resources
• Game pieces and answer key for self-assessment.
• Short-answer questions.
• Sample text.
• Rubric for written paragraph.

Purpose	
Standard	
Objectives	
Learning Goals	

Process

Products

Resources

THINK ABOUT IT!

Try your own Task Cycle with an upcoming lesson.

Conclusion

After you have finished your Task Cycle, go back and ensure that you have incorporated rigor throughout. Use the checklist below to help.

Checklist for Rigor	
Purpose	Are the standards, objectives, and learning targets at a rigorous level (measured against an outside standard)?
Product	Does your product incorporate higher order thinking and is it at a Level Three or higher on Webb's *Depth of Knowledge*?
Process	As you created the assessment, did you consider each aspect of rigor (high expectations, support and scaffolding, demonstration of learning)?
Resources	Are your resources challenging for students?

3

Linking Instruction and Assessment to Improve Rigor

Introduction

Rigorous instruction is integral to rigorous assessment. There are three times you will use assessments, and each has a particular type. Before the lesson, you'll use pre-assessments, during the lesson, formative assessments, and summative assessments at the end or after the lesson.

As we discuss instruction, we will look at several pre-assessment strategies for assessing prior knowledge before the lesson as well as some formative assessment strategies that can be used during the lesson. Then, in Chapter 4, you will see additional formative assessment strategies, and we'll turn our attention to summative assessment in Chapter 5.

Before the Lesson

Prior to teaching your lesson, it's important to gauge where students are in their knowledge of the topic. Although there are many formal diagnostic tools, such as pre-tests, we are going to look at four simple strategies you can use to assess students before you teach your lesson. Each is designed to encourage rigor through higher-order thinking.

3 Alike/Red Herring

I sometimes wondered what my students would learn if I didn't package everything together for them. One day, instead of telling them the objective for the day, I decided to let them figure it out. I named multiple cities, such as Raleigh, North Carolina, Sacramento, California, and Albany, New York. After a few seconds, one student shouted, "Hey, I know—those are all state capitals!" This is an easy way to determine what students already know, and it can be used at any grade level. A pre-kindergarten teacher can use it to introduce the color of the day, pulling items out of a box. A science teacher can use this strategy to introduce elements or subatomic particles.

To increase the rigor, Lindsay Yearta uses the "Red Herring" game with her students. She gives multiple examples that are linked, but students must identify the red herring—the one that does NOT belong. They must also justify their choice. Again, based on their responses, you can see how much they know, and by shifting the focus so the students generate the information, it is more rigorous.

If/Then Statements

Jayne Bartlett, author of *Outstanding Assessment for Learning in the Classroom* describes another rigorous method, which can be used to assess prior knowledge. Using if/then statements, students identify a connection and apply it.

**Sample Math If/Then Statements
on Multiplication and Division**

If $8 \times 40 = 320$, then calculate

1. 0.8×40
2. 8×4
3. 0.8×0.4
4. $320 \div 8$

She explains, "to extend this, you can ask pupils to determine a simple rule, 'If: taste → tasting, heat → heating, place → placing, time → timing, meet → meeting.' What is the rule?"

Once again, by requiring students to analyze the information on their own before you step in, you have increased the rigor.

Word Sorts

Word sorts also allow you to see how much students know. Give the students a set of word cards. Ask them to discuss the words in small groups and group them based on whether or not they fit in with the topic. Then, after reading a text, students revisit their word groupings and sort them again. To increase the rigor even more, preview the topic and have students generate related words on their own before reading the text.

Analyzing Webpages

A final way to assess prior knowledge is through analysis of webpages. Choose a sample webpage on a topic. Recreate it, but make several changes to add errors to the page. Ask students to evaluate the page you created to identify the mistakes. You'll be able to see what they know about the content.

THINK ABOUT IT!

Which of the before lesson activities would you like to try in your classroom?

During the Lesson

There are three important areas of classroom instruction used during instruction that are interrelated with assessment: Questioning, Self-Reflection, and Classroom Discussions. Each of these is a type of formative assessment as you will be able to determine students' knowledge through their comments.

Questioning

Questioning is a part of every rigorous classroom. Whether it is a teacher questioning students, students questioning a teacher, or students questioning each other, you see it integrated throughout almost every lesson. There are several general strategies you should incorporate as you question students.

General Questioning Strategies

- Provide adequate wait time.
- Call on a variety of students, not just those who raise their hands.
- Ask higher-order questions.
- If you ask a lower-level question, follow it up with a higher-order question.
- Encourage follow-up questions from students.
- If a student struggles with the answer, provide guidance and scaffolding rather than moving to another student.

Types of Questioning

Next, we'll look at four models for rigorous questioning. Although Bloom's Taxonomy is the most popular, the others provide additional insight into effective questioning.

Questioning Models

- Bloom's Taxonomy
- Costa's House of Questioning
- Marzano's Five Dimensions of Thinking
- Essential Questions

Bloom's Taxonomy

The original *Bloom's Taxonomy of Educational Objectives*, released in 1956, was designed to help teachers write objectives and create tests to address a variety of levels of understanding. In 2001, a group of researchers revised the original taxonomy to include a more rigorous progression.

By using the verbs and descriptors, you can plan objectives, activities, and assessments that allow students to gain different types of knowledge using a variety of processes. The widely used revised taxonomy is a complex but useful method for addressing all levels of questioning.

Revised Bloom's Taxonomy		
Level	*Description*	*Sample Question*
Remember	Retrieve knowledge, recognize, recall, locate, or identify.	Identify the villain in the story.
Understand	Clarify, paraphrase, illustrate, classify, categorize, summarize, predict, compare/contrast.	Summarize the character's encounter with the villain.
Apply	Apply to a familiar or unfamiliar task.	Choose your favorite scene and apply it to a real-life situation.
Analyze	Determine how parts relate, organize/outline, differentiate between relevant and irrelevant material.	Identify the three major plot points, providing evidence as to why those are the most relevant.
Evaluate	Make judgments based on evidence, judge, and critique.	Critique the actions of the villain.
Create	Generate, hypothesize, plan, produce.	Generate an alternate ending.

Costa's House of Questioning

Arthur Costa and Bena Kallick (2008), authors of *Learning and Leading with Habits of Mind*, provide a different model. It is a three-level, user-friendly, practical story house designed to describe the levels of questioning. I've observed this model used in several AVID (Advancement Via Individual Determination, www.avid.org) classrooms and it is effective for both students and teachers.

Costa's House of Questioning	
Level	*Verbs*
Level One (lowest)—gather information	Complete, identify, recite, define, list, select, describe, observe.
Level Two (middle)—process information	Compare, contrast, classify, sort, distinguish, explain, infer, analyze.
Level Three (highest)—apply information	Evaluate, generalize, imagine, judge, predict, speculate, if/then, hypothesize, forecast.

Samples for Costa's House of Questioning

Let's look at how Costa's House of Questioning can be applied in math, reading, and science.

Costa's House of Questioning for Math, Reading, and Science	
Math	*Reading*
Level One: Define *array*. Level Two: Compare and contrast an array to an area grid. Level Three: Make an array into a word problem.	Level One: Describe how the Big Bad Wolf destroyed the pigs' houses. Level Two: Compare and contrast the Three Little Pigs and the True Story of the Three Little Pigs. Level Three: Judge what you believe is the true character of the Big Bad Wolf and provide evidence to support your position.
Science	
Level One: Describe the approach you took to solve the problem. Level Two: Explain and sequence the steps of the science experiment used to arrive at a solution. Level Three: Hypothesize the outcome of the science experiment.	

Marzano's Five Dimensions of Thinking

In 1988, Robert Marzano and his colleagues released a framework called *Dimensions of Thinking*. It was designed to provide a way to look at different techniques of thinking.

Five Dimensions of Thinking	
Dimension	*Explanation*
Metacognition	Awareness and Control of Thinking
Critical and Creative Thinking	Critical: Analyzing and Assessing Evidence and/or Reasoning Creative: Applying Strategies
Thinking Processes	Multi-Step Thinking Skills: Problem-Solving, Research, and Decision-Making
Core Thinking Skills	Infer, Analyze, Compare, Summarize, Verify
Connecting Thinking to Content Knowledge	Apply to Specific Content Areas

As you can see from the chart, these thinking skills are very similar to those in other models, they are just framed differently. One key difference is that Marzano and his co-authors specifically address being aware of and controlling one's thinking (metacognition).

Essential Questions

Another way to look at questioning is through the seven defining characteristics of essential questions. Jay McTighe and Grant Wiggins (2013) explain the "aim is to stimulate thought, to provoke inquiry, and to spark more questions including thoughtful student questions, not just page answers. They are provocative and generative. By tackling such questions, learners are engaged in uncovering the depth and richness of a topic that might otherwise be obscured by simply covering it" (p. 3).

Seven Defining Characteristics of Essential Questions

1. Is open-ended.
2. Is thought-provoking and intellectually engaging.
3. Calls for higher-order thinking.
4. Points toward important, transferable ideas.
5. Raises additional questions.
6. Requires support and justification.
7. Recurs over time.

Let's look at a sample of their questioning framework in a lesson revolving around the September 11 attack on the United States.

Lesson Example Using the Seven Characteristics of Essential Questions	
Facet	*Sample Question*
Explanation	What are causes and effects of the 9/11 attacks?
Interpretation	Why do they hate us or is hate the right term?
Application	What might prevent another 9/11 or can we?
Perspective	What is the jihadists' story of 9/11?
Empathy	What motivates a suicide bomber?
Self-Knowledge	In what ways did 9/11 change me or my life?

Adapted from McTighe and Wiggins (2013) pp. 35–36.

THINK ABOUT IT!

Which of the models of questioning would help you improve your instruction?

Student Self-Assessment

In addition to the teacher asking questions of students, we also want students asking themselves questions for self-assessment. Encouraging students to assess themselves is more rigorous than the teacher providing all the assessment. Let's look at five strategies.

Self-Assessment Strategies

- Muddy Point Board
- Reflective Journals
- Video Confessionals
- Which Road Are You On?
- Triangle Reflection

Muddy Point Board

With the muddy point board, you designate an area in the room or a board for students to use to pin questions they have or muddy points that confuse them. You may have students do this at the end of lessons, or you may use them throughout the lesson. Not only does this provide you a perspective of their learning, it allows you to customize your instruction to their needs.

Reflective Journals

Another strategy for self-assessment is the use of reflective journals. Former middle school teacher Kendra Alston used journals with her students. She asked students to continually reflect on their learning in their *daybooks*, which are simple bound notebooks. Then she asked them to write a reflection on their learning at the end of the nine weeks. Some wrote about specific content they learned, other students reflected on how they learned.

Sample Reflections

Over this quarter, I've learned many things. One thing I've learned is teachers mean business and don't take kindly to slacking. I found that out the hard way. Another thing is that if you take the time to listen, teachers have a lot of helpful tips for passing the school year. (Justin, end of first nine weeks)

Something else that I learn [sic] would be about text organizers such as title, headings, caption/photograph, sidebars, and tags. Text organizers were not that confusing. At first I was getting tags and headings mixed up, but shortly I begin to understand them by the hands-on labs . . . I found that I understand the lessons better when we are able to do hands-on and get to experience and find what it is about ourselves. (Melissa, end of first nine weeks)

You can also use journals for students to reflect on specific information about their subject area. For example, in math, students might focus on explanations.

Sample Math Journal Prompts

- Explain how you solved an equation.
- Write about a time that you were really confused in math class. What did you do? Who did you get help from? How did you explain what was confusing you?
- Write about a time that you helped explain something to a classmate. What was your classmate having difficulty with? How did you help your classmate?
- Write everything you know about (choose a math topic).
- Write as many examples of a ratio that you can think of in 5 minutes.

Your students can write in their journals daily, weekly, or at the end of the month or grading period. Students can also keep their journals online in a blog format, or through GoogleDocs.

Video Confessionals

As described by Suzie Boss in an Edutopia blog entry, Ruth Farmer borrowed an idea from reality television. As Suzie describes:

> Farmer set up a self-contained "video confessional" in the corner of the classroom equipped with a stool and a video camera on a tripod, which she then surrounded with a curtain for privacy. When students had a free moment from their engineering investigations, they could duck behind the curtain, hit the Record button, and talk about how it felt to be an inventor.
>
> Farmer says the makeshift recording booth not only encouraged students to articulate what it means to think like an engineer or a scientist but also unexpectedly captured her students' feelings about the program. "From reading a written journal, I wouldn't have gotten the emotional attachment they had to their projects," Farmer explains. "On video, you can see them kind of puff up a little if they're excited or proud of what they're accomplishing."
>
> With her video-confessional approach, Ruth Farmer provided a fresh way of eliciting genuine student responses, which Charner-Laird says is the key to fruitful reflection. Kids can grow weary of "the reflection question" if teachers always present it to them the same way, she says.
>
> www.edutopia.org/student-reflection-
> blogs-journals-technology

Notice how the use of the "confessional" increases the rigor. Students must explain their thought processes, rather than simply demonstrating a basic understanding of the content.

Triangle Reflection

Finally, Melinda Crean, author of "Top Notch Teaching" (www.topnotch teaching.com) shares another way to have students reflect on where they are in the process of learning. Using triangles, she asks students to assess their level of learning.

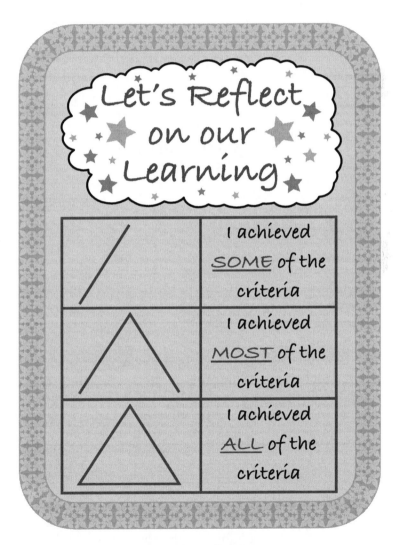

Triangle Reflection

Used with permission from Melinda Crean, Top Notch Teaching, http://topnotch teaching.com.

THINK ABOUT IT!

Which self-assessment strategy would help your students?

Discussions

The third integral instructional strategy is the use of classroom discussions. When students discuss content, we are better able to assess their learning by evaluating their questions and answers. It's also more rigorous, since each student is required to demonstrate learning. Let's look at three specific strategies for classroom discussion.

Strategies for Classroom Discussion

- Homework Circles
- Cubing
- Socratic Seminar

Homework Circles

One way to encourage discussion is through Homework Circles. Create an inside and outside circle of students facing each other (you can also use rows). Either ask students a question or use homework questions as prompts. They discuss the question with the person they are facing for 1–3 minutes. Next, the students in the outer circle rotate in a clockwise manner. Again, you ask a question, and students discuss it with their new partners. Continue to rotate and discuss until you finish the guided discussion.

Cubing

In a rigorous discussion, we want students to create their own questions, rather than us asking them all the time. With cubing, you put students into groups and give each group a cube like the sample on the next page. For a review of content, each member rolls the cube, and creates a question with the prompt that is showing. The other group members answer the question. Then the next student rolls the cube, and the game continues.

Story Cubing Pattern

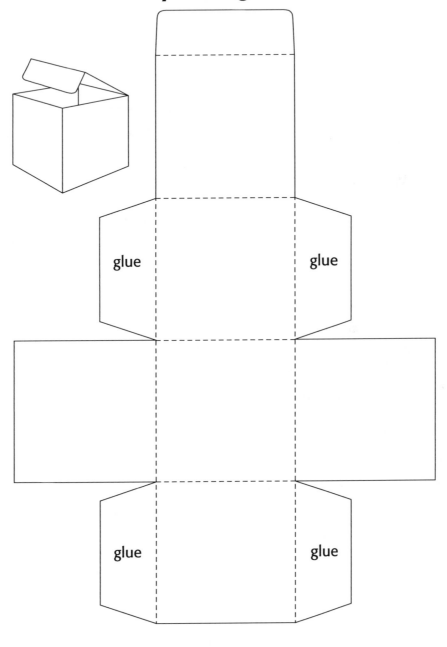

Sample Cube

glue

glue

glue

glue

With younger students, you may want to use the cube with the whole group. Students are grouped with a partner. Then, one student from the whole class rolls the cube, and everyone asks their partner a question starting with the prompt.

For older students, I have them log the questions they ask as well as the answers the group members give. Then, I take the papers up and use them for a whole class review. This also provides some accountability.

Socratic Questioning

When I was teaching, I learned about the Paideia seminar. A critical part of the seminar discussions was the notion of Socratic Questioning for student discussion. Although some questions were provided for guidance, I still struggled with asking questions at the highest levels. In 2006, Richard Paul expanded his earlier list of six types of Socratic Questions to nine categories (see next page). They are useful to guide students as they develop meta-cognition, or the concept of thinking about their own thinking.

In a Socratic seminar, the role of the teacher shifts to that of a facilitator and emphasizes each student's contribution to the discussion. As Marcia Alexander, a high school teacher explains:

> Paideia seminar has been the most successful teaching tool that I have used because it gives students the opportunity to demonstrate their knowledge and concerns about an issue that they can relate to. For example, I may have students read an excerpt written by Sojourner Truth, an African American ex-female slave, abolitionist, and speaker on women's rights. The discussion topic is discrimination and I create open-ended questions, such as "Does being illiterate make a person less intelligent?"

In her role as a facilitator, Marcia ensures that every student speaks at least once before she poses another open-ended question. The nature of the discussion requires that students actively listen to each other in order to respond appropriately.

Questions for a Socratic Dialogue	
Type of Question	*Samples*
Questions of Clarification	What do you mean by _____? What is your main point? Could you give me an example?
Questions that Probe Purpose	What was your purpose when you said? How do the purposes of these two groups vary? Was this purpose justifiable?
Questions that Probe Assumptions	What are you assuming? All of your reasoning depends on the idea that xxx. Why have you based your reasoning on xxx rather than xxx? Why do you think the assumption holds here?
Questions that Probe Information, Reasoning, Evidence, and Causes	What are your reasons for saying that? What led you to that belief? How could we go about finding out whether that is true?
Questions about Viewpoints or Perspectives	You seem to be approaching this issue from xxx perspective. Why have you chosen this perspective rather than that perspective? Can/did anyone see this another way?
Questions that Probe Implications and Consequences	What are you implying by that? Would that necessarily happen or only probably happen? If this and this are the case, then what else must be true?
Questions about the Question	How could someone settle this question? Can we break this question down at all? Why is this question important?
Questions that Probe Concepts	Do these two ideas conflict? If so, how? How is this idea guiding our thinking as we try to reason through this issue? Is this idea causing us problems? Which main distinctions should we draw in reasoning through this problem?
Questions that Probe Inferences and Interpretations	On what information are we basing this conclusion? Is there a more logical inference we might make in this situation? Given all the facts, what is the best possible conclusion?

THINK ABOUT IT!

Which discussion strategy would be helpful in your classroom?

Conclusion

Rigorous classroom instruction is directly linked to assessment. Assessing prior knowledge before your lesson and using questioning and facilitating classroom discussions during the lesson provide opportunities to deepen your assessment of student learning.

4

Formative Assessment for Rigor

Introduction

Formative assessment is one of the hottest buzzwords in education today. A Google search nets over a quarter of a million hits! This being the case, we must address its importance. I strongly believe that if we are going to truly support our students to higher levels, we must continually assess their learning and use that information to plan our future instruction.

Why is Formative Assessment Important?

According to Shirley Clarke in *Outstanding Formative Assessment*, the most powerful educational tool for raising achievement is formative assessment. She bases this on the work of John Hattie who, as we discussed in *Visible Learning*, synthesized over 900 meta-analyses of studies to determine what is effective in terms of increasing student learning and achievement. Let's look at five specific actions related to formative assessment. An effective strategy is measured by an effect size of more than .4.

Effect Sizes of Formative Assessment Strategies	
Influence Aspect	*Effect Size*
Assessment of literate students	1.44
Providing formative evaluation	.9
Classroom discussion	.82
Feedback	.75
Metacognitive strategies	.69

Four of these speak for themselves, but let's explore the notion of assessment literacy. This includes that students know what they are learning, can self-assess, and understand the success criteria.

What is Formative Assessment?

In 1998, Paul Black and Dylan William provided a clear rationale that using formative assessment effectively raises standards. In 2004, they and other researchers provided a fuller explanation of formative assessment in *Working Inside the Black Box: Assessment for Learning in the Classroom.*

> Assessment for learning is any assessment for which the first priority in its design and practice is to serve the purpose of promoting pupils' learning. It thus differs from assessment designed primarily to serve the purposes of accountability or of ranking or of certifying competence. An assessment activity can help learning if it provides information to be used as feedback, by teachers, and by their pupils, in assessing themselves and each other, to modify the teaching and learning activities in which they are engaged.
>
> (Black et al., 2004)

What does that mean to you as you consider your current assessments—whether they are tests, projects, homework, or a mix of items? Let's back up for a minute. Many assessments used in classrooms are final or culminating. In other words, they are used to evaluate a student. We will discuss that more in terms of summative assessments in Chapter 5. However, formative assessments are used to help a student and teacher adjust to improve learning.

W. James Popham (2008) points out that formative assessment is most effective when it is transformative. In other words, it transforms your teaching. In his book, *Transformative Assessment*, he describes four levels of implementation.

Popham's Levels	
Level One	Calls for teachers to use formative assessment to collect evidence by which they can adjust their current and future instructional activities.
Level Two	Deals with students' use of formative assessment evidence to adjust their own learning tactics.
Level Three	Represents a complete change in the culture of a classroom, shifting the overriding role of classroom assessment from the means to compare students with one another for grade assignments to the means to generate evidence from which teachers and students can, if warranted, adjust what they're doing.
Level Four	Consists of a school-wide adoption of one or more levels of formative assessment, chiefly through the use of professional development and teacher learning communities.

Popham (2008, p. ix).

Let's take a deeper look at Level Three of Popham's transformative assessment, which "represents a complete change in the culture of a classroom, shifting the overriding role of classroom assessment from the means to compare students with one another for grade assignments to the means to generate evidence from which teachers and students can, if warranted, adjust what they're doing" (p. ix).

Transformative Assessment		
Area	*From*	*To*
Learning Expectations	Substantial learning will occur for motivated students who possess adequate academic aptitude.	Substantial learning will occur for all students, irrespective of their academic aptitude.
Responsibility for Learning	The teacher, as prime instructional mover, is chiefly responsible for students' learning.	Students assume meaningful responsibility for their own learning and the learning of their classmates.
Role of Classroom Assessment	Formal tests generate data for comparing students and assigning grades.	Formal and informal assessments generate data for informing adjustments to the teacher's instruction and the students' learning tactics.

That is the ultimate goal of a classroom that is transformed based on formative assessment.

> **THINK ABOUT IT!**
>
> How does your assessment measure up and what steps would you take to improve your use of formative assessment?

Reflecting on Your Use of Formative Assessment		
Area	*Where You Are Now*	*Next Steps*
Learning Expectations		
Responsibility for Learning		
Role of Classroom Assessment		

Characteristics of Formative Assessment

If we accept that formative assessment is a critical part of our classrooms, then we need to determine what effective formative assessment is. Let's look at nine characteristics of effective formative assessment.

Effective FORMATIVE Assessment

1. Focus is improving teaching and learning.
2. Ownership of assessment shared by teacher and students.
3. Requires feedback to move learning forward.
4. Metacognition and self-assessment encouraged.
5. Activates students to be peer-assessors.
6. Takes place during instruction.
7. Identifies where students are and helps them move forward.
8. Variety of frequent assessments.
9. Examples of goals and grading criteria provided.

Focus is Improving Teaching and Learning

First, with effective formative assessment, the focus in on improving teaching and learning. It may seem self-evident that improving learning is a purpose of formative assessment, but it can also improve your teaching. We can learn from formative assessment where our instruction has been effective, and places where we need to improve.

Ownership of Assessment Shared by Teacher and Students

Because formative assessment impacts students and teachers, the ownership is shared. This is a shift from traditional assessment approaches that are teacher-focused. By including students in the process, students are more motivated, engaged, and more apt to learn.

Requires Feedback to Move Learning Forward

A critical aspect of formative assessment is feedback. In fact, it is so important, that I've devoted an entire chapter to it: Chapter 9. For the moment though, let's just note that, without giving feedback to students, there is no way for them to improve.

Metacognition and Self-Assessment Encouraged

As a part of student ownership, metacognition, and self-assessment are encouraged. Learning how to think about their own thinking is a skill students can learn, and it is one that is necessary for improved learning. If they can't assess themselves, students are always dependent on the teacher.

Activates Students to be Peer-Assessors

In addition to self-assessment, we should teach students to assess each other. Formative assessment works best in a collaborative environment, where the teacher collaborates with students, but also where students collaborate with each other. Providing opportunities for peer assessment, preceded by instruction on how to work together for assessment, is critical.

Takes Place During Instruction

Formative assessment also takes place during instruction, not afterward. If assessment is going to inform teachers and students as well as transform teaching, as W. James Popham says, it must occur during instruction. It is woven into the teaching and learning process, and is naturally integrated as opposed to being an add-on.

Identifies Where Students are and Helps Them Move Forward

Another characteristic of formative assessment is that it identifies where students are and helps them move forward. As we've already mentioned, the most effective formative assessment informs both teachers and students. The focus should be helping students learn, and this happens when you start where students are, and move them to new levels of learning.

Variety of Frequent Assessments

Next, formative assessment uses a variety of assessments, and they are used frequently. If we want to work with students to continually improve learning, the assessments need to occur on a regular basis. Additionally, instead of choosing to only use one type of assessment, such as an exit slip, effective teachers use a wide range of assessments to best understand students' strengths and weaknesses.

Examples of Goals and Grading Criteria Provided

Finally, it's important to provide clear goals for students so they understand what they are to learn. Without this understanding, they are not able to self-assess. You also need to provide examples of grading criteria, including rubrics, so that students gain a clear picture of expectations. Clarity in both goals and grading criteria are essential for students to share ownership of learning.

THINK ABOUT IT!

Which of the characteristics would make the most difference in your classroom if you focused on it?

Examples of Formative Assessment

Next, let's turn our attention to a variety of examples of formative assessments, which can be used throughout your lessons. Each of these can be rigorous when used appropriately, especially because they require students to demonstrate understanding and reflect on their own thinking. However, keep in mind you will need to encourage students to think at higher levels rather than settling for simple answers. Also, before we begin, consider two notes. First, we also discussed examples in Chapter 3, so you may want to refer back to those. Second, some formative assessments can be used as summative assessments.

Teacher-Directed Formative Assessments

Observations

An important formative assessment tool for teachers is the use of observations. Observations can be planned, or they can be spontaneous. In an observation, you simply observe what students are doing, and take notes for documentation. You may choose to observe for particular instructional behaviors, or you may simply observe to see what happens from a general standpoint.

The most effective observations are planned. For example, if you want to see a student's problem-solving ability, you would schedule time to observe the student during a science activity or experiment. The documentation, which may include simply taking notes, allows you to have a record of the student's skills at that point in time. By assessing it along with other formal and informal assessments, you gain a more accurate picture of the student's problem-solving abilities.

A second way to use observations is observing to plan your curriculum to best meet the needs of your students. Gaye Gronlund and Marlyn James, in their book *Focused Observations: How to Observe Young Children for Assessment and Curriculum Planning*, point out that after you observe students, you decide on the materials, activities, adult interactions, and peer involvement to meet the children's needs.

Running Record

Running records are one type of taking notes during an observation. It is exactly what the title describes. You keep a record of a student's activities and performances, running continually through the lesson or activities. Although they can be used as a diagnostic or summative assessment, we will address its use in a formative manner.

The main purpose of a running record is to note a student's performance. Although the typical form is written, I've also seen teachers use pictures or videos as a running record. Depending on the activity, pictures, or videos may be a more effective method of documenting what a student is doing.

Checklists

Checklists are a second strategy that can be used as a part of observations. Checklists can be simple yes/no tallies, or they can be open-ended for teachers to add notes.

Sample Mathematics Checklist	
Characteristic	*Notes*
Student demonstrates problem-solving ability.	
Student demonstrates persistence while solving problems.	
Student reflects on his/her thinking.	
Student shows applications of learning in real life.	

Retellings

Retellings are used in classes where students have read and processed a text, whether that is an article in science, a primary source in social studies, or a story in English/Language Arts. Students meet with the teacher to restate the text in their own words, so the teacher can determine how well they understand the text.

Interviews and Conferences

Similar to retellings, in interviews and conferences, the teacher meets with students to assess understanding of content. For either of these, the teacher plans a series of questions to ask a student about his or her learning. It's also important to stay flexible, and adjust questions during the interview or conference. These are probably used most often in writing situations, but they can be used with any subject area.

Sample Writing Conference Questions

- Please tell me a little about your writing.
- What do you think is going well?
- Show me an example of that.
- What are you struggling with?
- Show me an example.
- How do you think you can improve on your own?
- How can I help you?
- What are your next steps?

THINK ABOUT IT!

Which of these strategies is the most practical
for your classroom?

General Classroom Strategies

Classroom Discussions

Classroom discussions are an excellent way to gather data for formative assessment. First, as you ask questions, listen to students' answers. You can gauge how well students understand your content through their responses. Next, pay attention to the questions students ask. Again, this lets you know their depth of understanding, as well as their misunderstandings.

Let's look at a particular discussion strategy that is simple and helpful. You may already use a think-pair-share strategy, in which students think for a moment about a question you ask, pair with another student to discuss responses, then share out with the class.

There are two adaptations that can enhance this strategy. Douglas Fisher and Nancy Frey, in *Checking for Understanding: Formative Assessment Techniques for Your Classroom*, describe think-pair-square. Students still think about their answers and partner to discuss their thoughts, but then the join in with another pair to continue talking. This allows more conversation with a different group.

A second option is think-ink-pair-share (www.brilliant-insane.com/2015/02/twenty-creative-ways-check-understanding.html). In this, after students think about their answers, they write their response before they share. This can clarify understanding and allow for other students to read the notes.

Questioning

Questioning is a basic, and critical part of your classroom. We've already discussed questioning in Chapter 3, but let's add some information. For example, questions can be misused. Douglas Fisher and Nancy Frey share several reasons this can occur.

Misuses of Questioning

- Questioning rarely advances beyond the Initiate-Respond-Evaluate cycle.
- A minority of students dominate classroom questioning.
- Only teachers ask questions, rather than students asking questions also.

A fourth misuse I would add is the overuse of lower-level questions. While you may need to include some basic questions, it's important to move to higher-order questions. Let's look at how each of the levels of Bloom's Taxonomy relate to formative assessments (see the table on the next page). These move beyond simple questioning, but it is helpful to note the way higher levels of thinking and questioning differ from lower levels.

Specific Activities

Response Cards

Response cards are a practical strategy to see how much students understand about your content. The easiest way to use them is to give students a card with one possibility on the front and another one on the back (see p. 54).

Bloom's Taxonomy and Formative Assessment		
Bloom's Taxonomy	*Application*	*Sample Formative Strategies*
Knowing	Embedding learning in memory	Give three facts Quicktalk Quickwrite
Understanding	Fitting into prior learning; considering past knowledge by comparing and explaining	Think-Pair-Share Web diagrams
Applying	Using the learning in multiple and individualized ways	Application Cards Brainstorming Journaling
Analyzing	Making meaning by exploring and questioning	Chunking Corners Continuum with support for position taken Pros and Cons
Synthesizing/ Evaluating	Combining/connecting; putting ideas together; judging the ideas; critiquing	Continuum Feathers and Salt Gallery Self- and peer review Socratic questioning
Creating	Generating something new by planning and producing	Skits Cartoons Brochures Maps Quickdraw

Used with permission from Greenstein, L. (2010). *What teachers really need to know about formative assessment*. Alexandria, VA: ASCD.

Sample List of Duo Response Card Possibilities

Positive Responses

- I know!
- I understand!
- Agree
- True
- Fact
- Got it!
- Advantage
- I've got it!
- I like this!
- My mind is working!
- I feel great about this!

Opposite Responses

- I don't know!
- I don't understand!
- Disagree
- False
- Opinion
- No Clue
- Disadvantage
- I don't have a clue!
- I do not like this!
- My mind shut down!
- I am lost!
- This is not working for me!

Chapman, C. & King, R. (2005). *Differentiated Assessment Strategies: One Tool Doesn't Fit All.*

Invent a Quiz

Another way for students to demonstrate understanding is to create their own quiz about the content. Ask them to write 5–10 higher-order questions (you may need to give them question starters). Then, have them answer 1–2 of the questions.

Create Your Own!

You can also be creative in asking students to demonstrate understanding. Students could create comic strips, podcasts, videos, blog entries, Twitter feeds, or fake Facebook pages to show you what they know. As a bonus, these are fun and motivating for students.

You've Got Mail

In one of their blogs, Edutopia (www.edutopia.org/resource/checking-understanding-download) recommends using "You've Got Mail." As the author describes it,

> Each student writes a question about a topic on the front of an envelope; the answer is included inside. Questions are then "mailed" around the room. Each learner writes his or her answer on a slip of scratch paper and confirms its correctness by reading the "official answer" before placing his or her own response in the envelope. After several series of mailings and a class discussion about the subject, the envelopes are deposited in the teacher's letterbox.

Assume the Identity

Another option is to ask students to assume the identity of a character in a novel or story, a scientist, a historical figure, or the holder of a job, such as a nurse. They research the person, and craft a 2–5 minute monologue to perform. They must also be prepared to answer questions from the class, which requires them to demonstrate a high level of understanding.

Screencasting

With today's technology, it's important to assess what is happening with their use of technology. Screencasting allows students to record what happens on a particular device screen and add narration to the recording to make a video file. There are a variety of tools, depending on your hardware, that make this process easy to use.

Brain's Speech Bubble

Carolyn Chapman and Rita King, in their book *Differentiated Assessment Strategies; One Tool Doesn't Fit All* recommend an activity called The Brain's Speech Bubble.

The Brain's Speech Bubble

1. Make a large speech bubble.
2. Select a student to act as the speaker, or have the teacher explain his or her inside thinking while solving a problem.
3. Each time the person tells his or her thinking for a step, the bubble is held directly above the speaker's head. The speaker stands beneath the Brain's Speech Bubble as he or she verbalizes the brain's thinking for the class.
4. The speaker moves away from the speech bubble when not voicing his or her inside thinking to the class.

Before

- Is my mind focused on the task?
- Do I have what I need to get started?
- How do I get started?
- How can I organize my thoughts?

During

- Am I following directions?
- Does my answer make sense right here?
- Do I need a new category?
- Am I placing each piece of information in the right category?

It's an interesting way for students to demonstrate their thinking, as well as interact with the class.

Electronic Exit Tickets

You may already use exit slips or exit tickets, which are simple response forms for students to complete at the end of class. These can be as simple as "What did you learn" to more complex ones with multiple questions. However, with today's technology, there are a variety of ways to collect this information from your students.

Electronic Exit Slips

- Google Forms
- Plickers
- Twitter
- Socrative
- Geddit
- Poll Everywhere
- ExitTicket
- Voice Thread
- Lino
- Padlet

Wall of Knowledge

Angela Stockman, on the blog brilliant-insane.com, describes "Add a Brick to the Wall of Knowledge." She recommends creating a bulletin board, and giving students paper bricks. Ask them to write about what they have learned, and place (or staple) their bricks on the wall throughout the year. You could also give students boxes, and they could write new learning on the different sides of the box. Stack the boxes together to create a wall.

Metacognitive Strategies

A Bump in the Road

With a bump in the road, students reflect of their learning and identify 2–4 points where they hit bumps in the road, or struggles. Then, they partner with another student to see if they can work their way through their struggle.

Musical Notes/Color Clusters

Again, Carolyn Chapman and Rita King, in their book *Differentiated Assessment Strategies: One Tool Doesn't Fit All*, provide two ways for students to share how well they understand the content. Both require students to think about their own learning and identify their progress.

In musical notes, students use songs to identify their learning stage.

Musical Notes

Songs	Why?
"Celebrate"	Because I've "got it"
"I Can See Clearly Now"	Because I understand the information
"Leaving on a Jet Plane!"	Because I am "soaring" with this idea

Similarly, in color clusters, students label their learning progress through a series of colors.

Color Clusters

Example Key

- Purple = On the Launchpad
- Yellow = Cautious
- Green = Moving on up
- Blue = Soaring
- Red = Full Speed Ahead

THINK ABOUT IT!

Which of these strategies would you like to try in your classroom?

Conclusion

Formative assessment is a powerful tool for the rigorous classroom. It allows you to determine how much students understand, and where possible misconceptions lie. Formative assessment can be teacher-driven, general classroom strategies, specific activities, and metacognitive strategies. Through these, you are better able to transform your classroom instruction to enhance learning.

5

Rigorous Summative Assessments

Summative assessments are typically used at the end of a chapter, unit, or topic of study to assess students' overall understanding. They also form the basis for grades, particularly those used to compute a final grade for the report card. Although they can be used for diagnostic information, they differ from formative assessments in that their focus is different. There are more traditional summative assessments, which we will address in this chapter, and performance-based assessments, which are covered in Chapter 6.

Although valuable, we must be careful that we do not overuse or misuse summative assessments. Douglas Fisher and Nancy Frey, in their book, *Checking for Understanding*, share common misuses of testing, which include: narrowing the curriculum to only tested material; excluding instructional topics that are important but not tested, such as oral language; limiting learning to memorization or lower-level information; and devoting too much time to testing rather than learning.

Types

According to Larry Ainsworth and Donald Viegut (2006), there are four types of summative assessments: norm-referenced assessment, criterion-referenced assessment, selected-response assessment, and constructed-response assessment. The first two are typically used as standardized tests at the district, state, or national level. For classroom-based purposes, we'll look at the last two.

Selected-response assessments require students to select one response from a list provided by the teacher. Typically assessing lower levels of knowledge, these include matching questions, true-false items, fill-in-the-blank questions, and multiple-choice items.

Constructed-response assessments include short-answer and essay questions. In each of these, students must use their knowledge and skills to answer questions. It is easier to increase rigor through constructed-response questions.

Matching Questions

Matching tests are an quick and easy way to assess a wide range of student knowledge. However, it is difficult to assess at a higher level of rigor as most matching tests measure basic recall questions. Depending on the items, students can guess rather than truly demonstrate understanding.

What are the best strategies for developing quality matching tests? First, make sure there is one best option for each item you list. Ensure that students can see why the items match so that there is clear evidence students understand the link. Also, provide more examples than matching items. For example, if you have a list of vocabulary terms and a list of definitions, add one or two extra definitions to increase the rigor.

Tips for Writing Matching Tests

- Sequence options logically, such as alphabetically, chronologically, or in numeric order.
- Use numerals to label number options and letters for matching items.
- Keep all items and responses on the same page.
- Put definitions or explanations of left and words to choose on the right.
- Keep lists brief.

One specific type of matching test can increase rigor. The expanded matching format creates three columns that must be matched. It provides a better opportunity to measure what students know. In the following example, you'll also notice there are more choices than items, which requires students to narrow down the answer.

Directions: Match the person with the date and event.

Women's Historical Contributions		
Person	*Contribution*	*Time*
Fannie Lou Hamer Shirley Chisolm Marie Curie Alice Paul	U.S. Civil Rights activist and wife of Martin Luther King Jr. Ran for state senate on the platform of increasing minority employment. First African-American congressman (woman). Discovered the elements radium and polonium. Formed the Congressional Union (later named the National Women's Party) to raise public awareness for women's rights as a part of the Women's Suffragist Movement. Known as "Moses" and lead many slaves to freedom along the "Underground Railroad."	1800s 1910s 1920s 1950s 1960s 1970s

THINK ABOUT IT!

How might you use the expanded matching format with your students?

True–False Tests

True–false tests are an excellent way for students to determine accuracy of a statement, agree with opinions, and define terms. As with matching items, they are graded quickly and easily, and students can answer a wide range of questions in a short amount of time. However, once again, questions are typically low-level recall questions, and you may not be sure students understand the question or whether they are simply guessing. To combat this, and to increase the rigor, ask students to rewrite any false choices as true statements, which does require them to demonstrate a true understanding of the content.

In order to create effective true–false questions, it's important to avoid trivial statements and focus on core instructional content. Statements should be detailed enough that students must thoroughly read them, rather than glancing down to make a quick decision. Also, if your statement includes an opinion, provide the source for clarity and correctness.

Tips for Writing True–False Tests

- Use precise writing.
- Be sure choices are absolutely true or false (no in-betweens).
- Avoid always, never, none, or all.
- Keep all statements approximately equal length.
- Don't reflect a pattern (T,F,T,F . . .).
- Put T/F to circle so you don't have to guess at handwriting.
- Avoid negative statements.

Fill-in-the-Blank Questions

Fill-in-the-blank questions are also used to assess basic levels of knowledge. These are typically sentences with a blank, and students must fill in one or more words to complete it. As with matching and true–false tests, they are fairly easy to grade and they don't take much time to create. It is very difficult to find a way to make these questions rigorous. However, they do have their place, as long as you limit the use of these questions.

When creating a fill-in-the-blank question, be sure that your omitted words are critical to the content of the sentence. Otherwise, you end up with too many choices, and your students don't demonstrate understanding of the content.

Tips for Writing Fill-in-the-Blank Questions

- Put the blank near the end of the statement.
- Be sure you don't provide grammatical clues (such as He said . . .).
- Provide adequate space for response.
- Generally, only provide one blank.

One specific type of fill-in-the-blank item that is helpful, particularly for reading content (including content area reading), is the Cloze model. With this method, you provide students a text to read, generally one to three paragraphs, depending on the students. Leave the first and last sentence complete. For all remaining sentences, count to every fifth word, and put in a blank instead of the word. Students then read the selection and fill in all the blanks. It is one effective way to gauge a student's knowledge base.

Multiple-Choice Tests

Multiple-choice tests are probably the most used tests in classrooms across the nation. Although this is due in part to preparation for standardized tests, they are also easy to score. They also apply to a wide range of cognitive skills, including higher-order thinking ones. Finally, they are useful bcause incorrect answers, if written correctly, can help you diagnose a student's problem areas. Disadvantages include that the questions can't measure a student's ability to create or synthesize information, and that students can guess an answer.

One of the most important aspects of writing multiple-choice questions is creating the choices for the stem. If we are unclear, students can struggle. If we provide examples that are clearly off-topic, it makes it easier for them to guess.

Sample Multipe-Choice Questions and Guidelines

a. Avoid vague stems by stating the problem in the stem:

Poor Example
California:

   a. Contains the tallest mountain in the United States.
   b. Has an eagle on its state flag.
   c. Is the second largest state in terms of area.
   d. *Was the location of the Gold Rush of 1849.

Good Example
What is the main reason so many people moved to California in 1849?

   a. California land was fertile, plentiful, and inexpensive.
   b. *Gold was discovered in central California.
   c. The east was preparing for a civil war.
   d. They wanted to establish religious settlements.

---

b. Avoid implausible alternatives:

Poor Example
Which of the following artists is known for painting the ceiling of the Sistine Chapel?

  a. Warhol
  b. Flintstone
  c. *Michelangelo
  d. Santa Claus

Good Example
Which of the following artists is known for painting the ceiling of the Sistine Chapel?

  a. Botticelli
  b. da Vinci
  c. *Michelangelo
  d. Raphael

Used with permission from Steven Burton, Brigham Young University. Complete work here: https://testing.byu.edu/handbooks/betteritems.pdf.

Additionally, make the problem clear, and avoid repeating parts of your question in the answer. It's also important to avoid clues to the response in your question. Finally, although some recommend that you exclude the choices of *all of the above* and *none of the above,* if you include those, it can increase the rigor, since students have to make multiple decisions about the quality of responses.

Tips for Writing Multiple-Choice Questions

- Keep reading level of question stem simple
- Include a clear right or best answer
- Keep all choices a similar length
- Avoid grammatical cues (such as a plural word)
- Don't use never, always
- Avoid negatives
- Avoid patterns (a, c, d, b, a, c, d, b)

Although many multiple-choice questions measure lower-level understanding, you can increase the rigor. For example, in her book *How to Design Questions and Tasks to Assess Student Thinking*, Susan Brookhart provides a comparison of two multiple-choice items: one that is more basic and one that is at an increased level of rigor. In both, the student needs to know which character gives birth to twins, but notice the other information that must be understood in the second question.

Multiple-Choice Example One (less rigorous)

In E. B. White's essay "Twins," which character gives birth to twins?

A. The speaker's mother
B. A cow moose
C. A red deer
D. A shoe clerk

Multipe-Choice Example Two (more rigorous)

The following is from the first paragraph of the essay "Twins."

They stood there, mother and child, under a gray beech whose trunk was engraved with dozens of hearts and initials.

What does the sentence imply?

A. E. B. White is sympathetic to parents and children.
B. The deer were hiding from E. B. White and the other sightseers.
C. E. B. White is aware of both nature and the urban setting.
D. The graffiti interferes with E. B. White's enjoyment of the scene.

THINK ABOUT IT!

How can you improve the rigor and quality of your multiple-choice tests?

Short-Answer Questions

Short-answer questions are an expanded form of fill-in-the-blank. Responses are not as long as essays, but they usually include more than one sentence. Because students are required to create a response, they are more rigorous than the types of items we've already discussed. You'll need to build rigor into the context of your questions. Although more challenging to grade than matching, true–false, fill-in-the-blank, and multiple-choice questions, they are simpler than assessing essay questions.

Less Rigorous Example

What are two ways in which the vast desert regions of Southwest and Central Asia affect the lives of the people who live there?

More Rigorous Example

Which of the two deserts, the Gobi or the Karakum, is easier for surviving for those who might live there and why?

In order to write quality short-answer questions, be sure students know what they are expected to do. Keep reading level low, so that reading the question is not an obstacle to answering the questions. Finally, structure the question so that it requires a unique response.

Tips for Writing Short-Answer Questions

- Avoid negative statements.
- Keep writing spaces similar in length.
- Keep language free of clues.
- Ask direct questions.

One specific concern with both short-answer and essay questions is the vocabulary used in the questions. Earlier, I said to keep the reading level low, but what does that mean? First, avoid specialized vocabulary. In the prior example, it could be written as "Which of the two deserts, the Govi or the Karakum, is more palatable for those who might live there and why?" But the word *palatable* is particularly challenging for students, so the question uses the word *easier* instead. Additionally, for words such as *evaluate* and *analyze*, preteach the concepts prior to using them in a question.

Essay Questions

Essay questions, which are sometimes considered a type of performance assessment, are one of the most common assessments used in today's classrooms. Essay questions are extremely effective for measuring complex learning. Opportunities for guessing are removed, so you can truly measure what students understand. There are several disadvantages, including the amount of time to grade them, the subjective nature of grading, and the dependency of the answer on the student's writing ability.

When you are writing essay questions, crafting the question is particularly important. You want to be sure the complexity of the learning outcome is reflected in a clear, focused manner. It's also important to provide explicit instructions as to your expectations.

Tips for Writing Essay Questions

- Match question to standard or objective
- Build in opportunities to demonstrate relevant skills
- Avoid options for responses
- Write question at a low reading level

As with any questions, you can write items at a lower or higher level. In our case, we want to strive for rigorous questions as much as possible. Todd Stanley, in *Performance-Based Assessment for 21st Century Skills*, provides an excellent example of an essay question that he revised to a more rigorous version.

Standard Essay Question

What is the theme of "Goldilocks and the Three Bears"? Make sure to use details from the text to support this choice.

> ### Rigorous Essay Question
>
> What is the theme of "Goldilocks and the Three Bears"? Make sure to use details from the text to support this choice. "Goldilocks and the Three Bears" was written nearly 200 years ago. Justify whether this theme applies to today. Provide an example from modern life to validate your answer.

Notice that, although the first question (on the previous page) does require some higher-order thinking, the second one is at a more advanced level. It's very specific so that students know exactly what to do to demonstrate their understanding.

THINK ABOUT IT!

Choose an essay question you have written. Revise it to increase the rigor.

Conclusion

Summative assessments are typically used to measure students' overall understanding of concepts. They are either forced-choice tests such as matching, true-false, fill-in-the-blank, or multiple-choice questions, or constructed-response tests such as short-answer or essay questions. Each type has advantages and disadvantages; the key is to choose the one(s) that best meet your purpose. For each type of question, be sure to follow the principles of effective item writing.

6

Performance-Based Assessments to Enhance Rigor

Performance-based assessments are a type of summative assessments, but they differ from traditional testing. They are focused on students performing in some manner to demonstrate their understanding. Typically, performance-based assessments are more rigorous, because students must go in-depth to complete the performance, project, or portfolio.

Characteristics of Performance-Based Assessments

Larry Ainsworth and Donald Viegut provide an overview of performance-based assessments. They list ten characteristics that, taken together, give us a thorough picture of what quality performance-based assessments should accomplish.

Characteristics of Performance-Based Assessments

- Activity that requires students to construct a response, create a product, or perform a demonstration.
- Open-ended—may not always yield a single correct answer or solution method.
- Evaluations of student products or performances are based on scoring criteria (rubric) provided to students in advance of performance.

- Highly engaging for students; connects or applies content knowledge and skills to real-world situations.
- Promotes critical thinking—students must "show what they know" through the use of higher-level thinking skills.
- Student responses provide credible evidence that standards have or have not been met.
- Motivates all students to be proficient.
- Utilizes collaborative learning process but with individual accountability.
- Promotes peer- and self-assessment using scoring guide criteria.
- Offers multiple opportunities for students to revise work using scoring guide feedback.

THINK ABOUT IT!

Which of these characteristics is most important in your classroom?

Performance-based assessments can be broken down into three categories.

Types of Performance-Based Assessments

- Performances
- Project- and Problem-Based Learning
- Portfolios

Performances

Performances encompass a wide range of activities, some of which can be incorporated in project- and problem-based learning and portfolios. The main distinguishing characteristic is that students perform in some manner to demonstrate understanding.

For example, Kendra Alston shared a performance activity she experienced when she was taking a high school social studies class. She wasn't excited to study the 1920s and 1930s, but her teacher, Mr. Baldwin told them he was giving a *show me what you know* final exam. "He didn't care how you showed it, as long as you showed what you know. Things flashed before my eyes, but I was into theatre. So I researched the vaudeville circuit at time and found Bessie Smith in theatre. She was a blues singer who sang in speakeasies; and I learned about the 20s and 30s through her eyes. On day of the exam, I came in singing, staying in character. He asked questions and I answered based on what Bessie Smith would have said." Notice how rigorous the assessment was. She had to demonstrate far more understanding than simply answering a question.

Other Sample Performances

- Oral Presentations
- Reader's Theater
- Exhibitions
- Essays
- Multimedia Presentations
- Debates
- Role-Playing
- Experiments

Now, let's look at three additional samples of rigorous performances, one for each grade range. First, here's a sample assessment for high school math. Compare this to a test that, for example, asks students to evaluate a set of linear equations and interpret them. Which provides a more rigorous assessment?

Sample High School Mathematics Performance Tasks

PARCC High School Task: Golf Balls in Water

Part A: Students analyze data from an experiment involving the effect on the water level of adding golf balls to a glass of water in which they:

- Explore approximately linear relationships by identifying the average rate of change.
- Use a symbolic representation to model the relationship.

Part B: Students suggest modifications to the experiment to increase the rate of change.

Part C: Students interpret linear functions using both parameters by examining how results change when a glass with a smaller radius is used by:

- Explaining how the y—intercepts of two graphs will be different. Explaining how the rate of change differs between two experiments.
- Using a table, equation, or other representation to justify how many golf balls should be used.

Herman, J. L., & Linn, R. L. (2013). On the road to assessing deeper learning: The status of Smarter Balanced and PARCC assessment consortia (C RESST Report No. 823). Los Angeles: University of California, National center for Research on Evaluation, Standards, and Student Testing as found in Hammond, Next Generation Assessment: Moving Beyond the Bubble Test to Support 21st Century Learning.

Next, let's look at a middle school science example.

Middle School Science Example

Using their knowledge of past catastrophic events that have affected the Earth and life on Earth such as earthquakes, volcanic eruptions, weather devastations, and asteroid contact, students must predict the next catastrophic event that is likely to occur. They must also support their prediction with a minimum of three sources other than the classroom text. Students will present this information in the form of a live classroom presentation or by electronic submission in a form the entire class can review such as Blackboard or Canvas.

Finally, we turn our attention to an upper elementary art example.

THINK ABOUT IT!

Create your own performance assessment.

Project-Based and Problem-Based Learning

Project-Based Learning and Problem-Based Learning are effective strate-gies for helping students apply their learning and demonstrate their problem-solving skills. Let's start by looking at project-based learning, and then turn our attention to problem-based learning.

Projects vs. Project-Based Learning

Do you remember doing projects when you were a student? I do. My teachers typically assigned everyone a standard project; we completed them and turned them in, and then received a grade. It wasn't very rigorous.

According to the TeachThought staff (www.teachthought.com), there is a difference between projects and project-based learning. For example, projects can be done independently at home, but project-based learning requires teacher guidance and collaboration.

Projects vs. Project-Based Learning	
Projects	*Project-Based Learning*
Teacher works mainly after the project is complete.	Teacher works mainly before the project starts.
May or may not be relevant.	Are relevant to students' lives or future lives.
Based on directions and are done "like last year."	Based on driving questions that encompass the learning and establish the need to know.
Are closed; every project has the same goal (such as create a diorama of the Alamo).	Are open-ended; students make choices that determine the outcome and path of the research (such as design a fortification that would take your community through a bio-attack).

Examples of Project-Based Learning

Jessica Guidry designed an ecology unit for her science classroom that utilizes project-based learning. Her students were introduced to the unit with the following task:

> You are an ecologist from Rock Hill, South Carolina. Recently, members of the United Nations have come together and decided that they must eliminate one biome to make room for the world's growing human population. You and a group of your peers have decided to take a stand. You will each choose one biome to present to the United Nations in New York City this April. It is very important that you persuade the members of the UN to keep your chosen biome alive! The UN has asked that you write a persuasive essay to present to the audience. They also asked that you bring visuals and information about your references. You must be sure that you include how your biome benefits the world population. You need to include information about the habitats, populations, animals, plants, and food chains of your biome.

Throughout the unit, she integrated a variety of other open-ended activities, such as creating a flip book on their biome, participating in a debate, and creating food chains/webs in addition to the regular mix of lecture, guided discussion, and laboratory activities. The overall focus on an open-ended project for groups, however, was the driving force for the unit.

A teacher in one of my workshops shared an example of project-based learning for teaching health in a secondary school. She asked students to create a "How to Be Healthy" campaign. First, they were to gather data about student absenteeism, including the reasons students were absent. They could use surveys, interview students, or ask teachers for overall numbers of absences.

Next, they chose a specific focus area of health. They researched information about the health of their city, state, or region. They looked at national or county health rankings, published data about numbers of flu or measles cases, or any other information they could find. The center for Disease Control and the state and local health departments were an excellent source of information.

Finally, each group created a campaign to teach healthy habits to students. After choosing their targeted age group (such as elementary school or intermediate grades), they chose a medium (web-based, multimedia, etc.) and developed a campaign. The groups presented their finished projects at the end of the semester.

Other Sample Projects

Select an insect mascot for your school. Research the insect and create a realistic mascot. Craft a multimedia presentation to present your creation.

Choose an issue in history, such as the Civil Rights Movement or the Equal Rights Movement. In groups, create and perform an original composition. Depending on the age of your students, they might draw a cartoon strip, write a song, or create a video.

Imagine you are a group of spies. Your job is to crack a coded message that has been intercepted from the enemy detailing the plans for an attack. Your group needs to crack the code, find the coordinates of the attack location and any other plans, and send a coded message to your supervisor.

Your job is to use everyday items to create a new invention to present to a group of venture capitalists, who will decide whether or not to fund you. Design your invention and develop a creative way to present it.

Problem-Based Learning

Problem-based learning (PBL) is "an inquiry process that resolves questions ... Student inquiry is very much an integral part of PBL and problem resolution" (John Barell, 2016, p. 3).

You may be thinking that PBL sounds a lot like project-based learning. The main difference is that in project-based learning, the teacher directs the questions and assigns the final product. In problem-based learning, the students are more self-directed and come up with many of their own questions, which is even more rigorous than project-based learning.

I recently visited a kindergarten classroom using PBL. Students were learning about various colors, and one student asked, "Are there other colors we don't know about?" The teacher took advantage of this question and asked students to work with a partner to create their own colors. Students had total flexibility with how they determined their color, how they would explain the color to the class, and how they would show and/or demonstrate the new color. As one student said to me, "It was awesome to answer our own question!"

Darrin Baird used problem-based learning with his high school marketing students. As he said, "I turned the control to students, rather than me." One day, he brought a box of Cheerios to class. As he discussed marketing ideas for different products, the students began to plan other purposes for Cheerios. They worked in small groups to discover purposes for the cereal, as well as ways to market the product. This open-ended activity enabled students to solve a complex problem of interest to them that was also linked to their class standards.

Although there are various models for posing problems, one that is particularly valuable is the KWHLAQ (Barell, 2016). Students, often in small groups, work through all phases of the model to solve a problem.

KWHLAQ Model	
K	What do we think we already KNOW?
W	What do we WANT to find out in order to solve the problem?
H	HOW and where will we find the answer?
L	What do we think we will LEARN? What did we LEARN?
A	How will we APPLY what we learned?
Q	What are our QUESTIONS now that we have finished our inquiry?

Adapted from Barell (2016).

Sample Problem-Based Learning Experiences

In an area secondary school, there was an accident that occurred near the school. Students wanted to prevent future accidents, so they worked in groups to develop a safety plan for drivers. In addition to creating safety information, such as brochures and a short video, groups also worked together to petition for a stoplight at the intersection to make the area safer.

After reading *The Moon Book* by Gail Gibbons, students in an elementary classroom asked, "How long would it take to go to the moon?" In groups, they decided on a method of transportation, such as a rocket or on a light beam, researched the time it would take to make the trip, created a list of needed supplies, and then described their travels. Some wrote a book, others produced a simple video, but all combined creativity with information to demonstrate their learning.

Remember, with problem-based learning, there is more control with the students. They generate questions based on a standard or essential question, and then discover the answer through their own research. This doesn't mean that you allow them to stumble through the project on their own; you'll need to guide and facilitate as well as frame parts of the activity to provide a loose structure. As an end result, students choose to demonstrate their understandings in a creative way such as with videos, blogs, reports, models, experiments, or metaphors.

THINK ABOUT IT!

Choose a topic you are teaching in an upcoming unit. Create either a project-based assignment or a problem-based assignment you can use with your students.

Portfolios

Portfolios can incorporate performances and project- and problem-based learning. A portfolio is a collection of artifacts a student presents, either to peers, the teacher, parents and family members, or all of these groups. There are two types of portfolios.

Types of Portfolios

- Best Work
- Growth

Both are effective. You choose which one you want to use based on your purpose. Do you want students to show off their finished products, which includes more summative assessments? Or do you want students to show how they have grown over time, which might include more formative assessments.

The key with portfolios is organization. When I was a teacher, I attempted to use portfolios with my students. All I ended up with were folders packed with assignments. I didn't set any parameters for collecting work, so my students put everything in the folder. I also didn't set an authentic purpose for the portfolio, so they collected dust.

What I learned was that it's critical to plan for portfolios.

Planning for Portfolios

- Plan Purpose
- Plan Process
- Plan Product Sharing
- Plan Resources

Plan Purpose

First, you should plan for the purpose of the portfolio. In other words, why do you want students to collect artifacts? Is it so students can review their progress throughout the year? Perhaps you simply want students to document their understanding. Or is it to be used for parent conferences? Finally, perhaps you want to be able to grade a set of overall work from each student.

Plan Process

Next, it's important to decide upon a process for the portfolios. How will they be collected? Do you want electronic versions, print ones, or a combination? How often will artifacts be collected? Who will select the artifacts—the student, you, or both? All of these questions must be answered in advance. And remember, the artifacts should be those that reflect rigorous assignments.

Plan Product Sharing

A third consideration is how students will share their portfolios. Without the opportunity to showcase their work, there is no authentic value for students.

Opportunities to Share Portfolios

- Peers
- Teachers
- Parents/Families
- Public

Plan Resources

Finally, what resources will you need to make your plan happen? If you are using paper portfolios, you may need folders, crates, notebooks, or large envelopes. If you are planning for electronic portfolios, you'll need to consider software that is helpful, website access and space, or hard media such as a flash drive.

As a part of resources, consider those that are non-material. For example, one such resource is your time. How much time will you spend planning and organizing portfolios? How much will you spend maintaining and assessing them? Another consideration is the class time it will take to collect the artifacts. It is time well spent, but you need to plan for it.

THINK ABOUT IT!

How might you use portfolios in your classroom?

Conclusion

Performance-based assessment is a type of summative assessment that focuses on students demonstrating their understanding through performances, project- or problem-based learning, or portfolios. Through these types of alternative assessments, students must show their learning in a more rigorous, in-depth manner.

7

Differentiated Assessments to Increase Rigor for All Students

Differentiation is a key concept in today's educational environment. We have an ever-widening range of students, which requires that we adjust our instruction and assessment to meet their needs while still ensuring rigor for each of them. Effective differentiated assessment means that you customize your assessment to best meet the needs of every student. As Rick Wormeli points out in the title of his book, *Fair Isn't Always Equal*. Therefore, you may need to provide different, yet rigorous assessments for different students.

Myths of Differentiation of Assessments

Are there misconceptions about differentiated assessment? Yes. Carol Ann Tomlinson and Tonya Moon describe two common myths. First, they point out that many teachers believe that differentiation means having different goals for different students. However, true differentiation provides multiple pathways and support systems to the same content goals. In other words, you are assessing how each student is making progress toward the same standard.

Second, they say that some believe that differentiation means grading struggling students "easier" and advanced students "harder." Instead, all students should be graded against the same criteria. However, the classroom should provide an environment that allows each student to achieve the criteria, and, for some students, to exceed the criteria.

Frameworks for Differentiation of Assessments

Let's look at two frameworks for differentiating assessments. The first comes to us from Carol Ann Tomlinson and Tonya Moon. They propose that differentiated assessment can be based on a student's readiness, interests, and learning profile.

Differentiation Criteria

Readiness: A student's proximity to specified learning goals
Interest: Passions, affinities, kinships that motivate learning
Learning Profile: Preferred approaches to learning

As a caution, you may know that there are researchers, particularly John Hattie, who have pointed out that achievement is not necessarily impacted by learning styles. However, looking at a student's preferred approach may be beneficial in differentiation.

What do these criteria look like in practice? Let's look at examples of products by each of the criteria.

Examples of Products by Differentiation Criteria

Readiness	Interest	Learning Profile
A middle school teacher provides all students with models of effective student products from prior years to help them analyze what quality work looks like. Although all of the examples demonstrate proficiency with KUDs, students who are more advanced with the content examine models at a higher degree of sophistication.	High school students studying Robert Frost's "Road Not Taken" use the life of a famous person or well-known character from movies or literature to demonstrate parallels between the events in the poem and in the life of the person they chose.	Elementary students use meteorological data to make a forecast for the week ahead in their town. All students must predict the weather and explain their prediction. They may write and illustrate the forecast for the local paper, present the forecast for TV, or create a weather map that depicts their forecast.

Tomlinson, C. & Moon, T. (2013), *Assessment and Student Success in a Differentiated Classroom*.

Differentiating Homework

Second, Cathy Vatterott provides a different model for differentiation of homework. She points out there are three ways to differentiate homework to meet the needs of a variety of learners.

Differentiating Homework

- Differentiate by difficulty or amount of work
- Differentiate by amount of structure or scaffolding
- Differentiate by learning style or interest

When we look at these, we see clear differences from the prior framework. First, you can differentiate with the difficulty level or amount of work. Christy Matkovich, a middle school math teacher, uses learning centers to differentiate the small-group activities she utilizes in her classroom. In these activities, she differentiates by difficulty level.

At each center there are four different folders, with a number (one through four). When it is center time, if a child sits at a one in his or her group, then he or she may choose a center and complete the activity in folder number one at that center. If a child sits at the three spot in his or her group, then during center time, he or she may choose a center and complete the activity in the folder number three at that center. When preparing activities for each center, I make sure that the concept for all four folders is the same. For example, at center number one, everyone may be working on concepts that involve order of operations. However, the level of difficulty varies based on the folder number. Folders one and two are basic activities, and folders three and four are enrichment activities. This arrangement allows me to challenge the higher-level students and do some remediation for the lower-level students.

Next, you can differentiate by the amount of structure or scaffolding you provide to students. When I was teaching, some of my students understood descriptive writing, and others who didn't. So I created a folder game. Each group of students was given a folder with a picture from a newspaper or magazine article pasted inside. Students were directed to look at the picture. Then, individually, each student wrote as many words as possible about the picture, one word per Post-It note. Since they are only writing words, the tiny sticky note is adequate.

Next, students talked to each other, using all their words to create a sentence about the picture. Usually, someone asked to add words, such as "the" or "and," or to add punctuation, which gave me a quick teachable moment to discuss grammar and sentence structure. Then I told them they could write anything they needed on more notes. Each student also made a copy of the words they didn't use.

For homework, students then individually wrote a descriptive paragraph about the picture. For the students who didn't know how to begin, they had a group sentence for a starting point. For those who needed it, they had a customized word bank of leftover words to use in the paragraph. This provided additional support without changing the activity.

Finally, you can differentiate by learning style or interest. My favorite strategy for this is to use tic-tac-toe boards (see table on the next page). At the end of a unit, rather than assigning the same project for all students, give them a tic-tac-toe board with nine possible assignments. Students choose three to create tic-tac-toe. You can structure the assignments so that some are more rigorous than others, but be sure that each one has some rigor built in.

THINK ABOUT IT!

Choose a homework assignment you have planned.
Adapt it based on one of the three options listed in this chapter.

Tiering

A third common method of differentiation, which has become popular as a part of Response-to-Intervention, is tiering. Tiering is differentiating instruction and assessment up and down to meet the challenge level of the students. As Rick Wormeli points out in his book *Fair Isn't Always Equal*, you start tiering by expecting everyone to demonstrate mastery of the standard. Then, you raise the challenge level for advanced students, and provide additional support for the lower tier. In this case, the primary determinant of the differentiation is the readiness level of the student. The minimum tiering goal is three tiers: a standard tier, one above that, and one below that. However, you may have more tiers, or you may not have a particular tier, depending on your students. You also may not tier every aspect of the lesson.

For a lower tier, we need to add more structure and support. This can take the form of additional time, layered levels of practice, more modeling, reading an easier book before we read the grade-level text on the test so we have additional background knowledge and vocabulary skills, or using graphic organizers to help us understand content. However, providing additional support does not mean lowering the level of rigor; you should still ask higher-order questions.

Sample High School Science Tic-Tac-Toe		
Create a T-chart to share how structures such as carbohydrates, lipids, proteins, DNA and RNA are related to their functions in plants and animals. | Structure	Related to Animal Cell Function	Related to Plant Cell Function
DNA		| Justify your responses with at least two pieces of evidence.	Create a 3D model of a plant or animal cell.	Create a virus with all of the attributes and describe how that virus must use living cells to reproduce. Use your text and at least two other sources to support your description.
Using at least three sources, research the effects the environment has on plant and animal cells to include effects such as diseases. Create a presentation to share your findings with your classmates.	Write a two-voices poem for animal and plant cell functions. In your reflection, provide support for your statements.	Create a game about plant and animal cells.
List all of the specialized structures within the animal cell such as DNA or ribosomes and describe the structure's function. Next, predict what would happen if one of those structures didn't exist. Support your prediction with evidence.	Create a Venn Diagram to compare the differences and similarities of plant and animal cells. Next, create your own entity that has cells. Add the third circle to your Venn diagram and complete it.	Create a RAFT where you choose the Role, Audience, and Format. Your Topic will be to explain how plant cells and animal cells meet the same life needs such as produce, transport and modify proteins.

For the more advanced tier, we need to increase the assessment complexity. Rick Wormeli provides suggestions.

Increasing Assessment Complexity

- Manipulate information rather than echo it.
- Increase the number of variables that must be considered.
- Use or apply content/skills in situations not yet experienced.
- Work with advanced resources.
- Identify the bias or prejudice.
- Deal with ambiguity and multiple meanings or steps.
- Critique something against a set of standards.
- Work in more abstract concepts and models.

Note that although these examples are for an advanced tier, you should consider those that are applicable for the standard tier, as each is an example of a rigorous assignment.

Now, let's look at a sample set of tiered assignments for a primary grade classroom. One adaptation I would recommend for all levels is to ask students to provide evidence for their responses, in order to increase the rigor.

Sample Tiering Assignments for Primary Grades: Completing a Character Map	
Tier One	Describe how the character looks, what the character says, how the character thinks or acts, the most important thing to know about the character.
Tier Two	Describe what the character says or does, what the character really means to say or do, what goals the character has, what the character would mostly like us to know about him or her, what changes the character went through.
Tier Three	Describe clues the author gives us about the character, why the author gives us these clues, the author's bottom line about this character.

Wisconsin RTI Center, www.wisconsinrticenter.org/assets/files/Family%20 Engagement%20Module/Activity%203a_Tiered_Assignments.pdf.

THINK ABOUT IT!

Choose an upcoming lesson. Create three tiers of activities and implement them with your students.

Student Self-Assessment of Tiering Levels

Although you will use strong pre-assessments to determine the best learning levels for your students, it helpful to ask students to self-assess their progress during the assignment or assessment. Marcia B. Imbeau (www.iag-online.org/resources/2014_handouts/Imbeau_tiered.pdf) provides a set of questions students can use to determine if they are working at the correct level. You'll see an excerpt of her lists below.

Questions for Self-Assessment		
Too Easy	*On Target*	*Too Hard*
• I already know how . . . • This is a cinch . . . • I'm coasting . . . • I'm bored . . . • No big effort necessary . . .	• I know some things . . . • I have to think . . . • I have to persist . . . • I hit some walls . . . • I have to re-group . . . • I feel challenged . . .	• I don't know where to start . . . • I can't figure it out . . . • I'm missing key skills . . . • I feel frustrated . . . • This makes no sense . . .

Used with permission from Tomlinson, C. A. (2013, July). University of Virginia Summer Institute on Academic Diversity Keynote Strand. Charlottesville, VA.

Differentiated Grading for Students with Special Needs

A common assessment challenge when differentiating for students with special needs is grading. How can we ensure rigorous grading without defeating students if they don't meet the standards? Should I grade effort? What should count and how do I grade that?

These are difficult questions, and I do not have a perfect solution. Ideally, we would use report cards that allow us to put two grades: one that represents how students perform compared to the grade-level standards and one that shows how they are performing at their level. Unfortunately, many districts do not allow for this. So what are our alternatives?

Thomas Guskey, in *Practical Solutions for Serious Problems in Standards-Based Grading*, suggests five categories that allow you to customize a grading system to meet individual needs in a standards-based system.

Five Categories to Customize a Standards-Based Grading System

1. Considering progress on IEP goals.
2. Measuring improvement over past performance.
3. Prioritizing assignments or content differently.
4. Including indicators or behavior effort in the grade.
5. Modifying the weight or skill for grading.

Teachers like this process, because it helps students feel successful when they otherwise might not. However, students may misinterpret their grades, believing they haven't earned them; they simply received a grade for who they are.

Based on those concerns, let's look at a second model by Jung and Thomas Guskey. This is designed to allow classroom teachers and special needs teachers to work together to grade in a standards-based environment.

Five-Step Inclusive Grading Model

1. Determine if the accommodations or modifications are needed for each grade-level standard.
2. Establish the appropriate modified standard for each area requiring modification.
3. Outline additional goals pertinent to the child's academic success.
4. Apply equal grading practices to the appropriate standards.
5. Clearly communicate grades' meanings.

In this five-step inclusive grading model, students are still measured to the standards, but with appropriate accommodations and modifications for the individual student.

Grading students with special needs is challenging, and ultimately, you must work with other teachers in your school, including the teacher of special needs students, to determine the best way to grade within your school's, district's, and state's parameters. This is also true as you work with grading other struggling learners.

Differentiated Grading for Gifted Students

Differentiating grading for gifted students is another challenging area, one for which there are no clear solutions. You might follow some of the same strategies as for special needs students (i.e. customizing the grade, noting on the report card where they are based on grade-level standards and what they score compared to more rigorous standards). Although not a solution, there are two key questions for you to consider as you grade gifted students:

1. Do students show mastery of grade-level standards as well as more rigorous standards?
2. Are you clearly communicating to the student and parents/ families what the student is and is not able to do?

THINK ABOUT IT!

Consider how you currently grade or assess students with special needs and gifted students. What changes, if any, would you like to make?

Conclusion

Differentiation and rigor are key aspects of a classroom with a diverse group of students. There are several frameworks for differentiating assessment in your classroom. Additionally, you may consider how to grade students with special needs and those who are gifted. Although differentiated assessment is challenging, the benefits for student learning are worth it.

8

Grading in a Rigorous Classroom

Grading

Grading is one of the most challenging parts of a rigorous classroom. Many of the aspects of grading, such as whether to grade homework, are individual choices for a teacher. When making grading decisions, always start by considering your purpose.

Purposes of Grading

What is your purpose for grading a particular assignment? Are you setting a benchmark to see which of your students have met a standard? Or are you evaluating their progress, so you can make decisions about your future instruction? One of my problems the first year of teaching was that I didn't have a good answer to that question. In fact, if you asked me why I was grading something, my answer would have been, "So I can have enough grades for the report card."

There are several purposes of evaluation. Schools use evaluation to make decisions about placements, particularly in ability-leveled classes or for consideration of promotion to the next grade level. The process of moving students to higher levels requires some type of evaluative judgment. Teachers also use evaluative data to group students and plan for instruction tailored to specific needs. This is one of the most important uses of evaluation. If you collect information about a student, but don't use it to plan what to teach next (or what to reteach), what use is it? Closely linked to this purpose is the notion of using evaluative data to provide feedback to students, so they can improve. Both purposes require that you plan the type of assessment used to ensure you gain the specific information you need to make decisions.

A final use of grades is to externally motivate students. Some students respond well to this form of motivation; grades are just a higher-stakes version of receiving a pizza for reading books. You simply can't get away from the fact that grades provide external pressure on students. Some thrive in this situation; others suffer. Parents and/or family members may complicate the situation if they value the grades differently or more than the student. No matter your purpose, an overemphasis on grades will undermine learning.

Let's take a look at key indicators of effective grading.

THINK ABOUT IT!

What is your purpose for grading?

Indicators of Effective Grading

Effective GRADING Indicators

- Grade According to Your Policy.
- Rubrics Can Be Helpful.
- Align Grading to Assessment.
- Don't Count Attendance, Effort, or Behavior.
- Involve Students in Grading.
- Never Give Zeroes.
- Grade for Quality, not Completion.

Grade According to a Policy

In a rigorous classroom, teachers provide a clear grading policy so that students and parents know what to expect. Ideally, you would work together with teachers at your grade level, in your team, or in your department so there is consistency. However, that may not be possible. Grading policies should be communicated early in the school year, ideally in writing. They are also important for all grade levels, including the primary level. Remember to match the language and format of the policy to the level of your students.

Rubrics Can Be Helpful

Rubrics are written descriptions of the criteria used to grade an assignment. They show students what they are expected to do. Todd Stanley in his book *Performance-based Assessment for 21st Century Skills* provides six steps to creating rubrics.

Let's look at a sample excerpt for a science rubric.

Science Project Rubric			
	Exemplary	*Acceptable*	*Not Yet (Do Over)*
Problem and Hypothesis	• Problem is new meaningful, well researched. • Hypothesis is clearly stated in the "IF . . . THEN" format.	• Problem is meaningful and researched. • Hypothesis is stated.	• Problem is addressed vaguely with little research support. • Hypothesis is unclear or not stated.
Research Support	• Research is thorough, specific, and includes many examples. • All ideas are clearly explained. • History, biology, and pros and cons are fully addressed.	• Research has some specifics and examples. • Most ideas are explained. • Student mostly addresses the history, biology, and pros and cons.	• Research has little specifics and few examples. • Two or fewer ideas are explained. • Student doesn't address all or any areas: history, biology, and pros and cons.
Variables	• Variables have been identified, controls are appropriate, in place, and explained. • Sample size is appropriate and explained.	• Variables have been somewhat identified, controls are appropriate and in place. • Sample size appropriate.	• Missing variables or controls. • Sample size is not appropriate or is not considered.

Align Grading to Standards

It's important to align your grading to your standards, goals, and objectives. That may sound basic, but I've often seen an assignment that called for certain outcomes based on the standards, but the grade was based on other criteria. How frustrating for a student. For example, I spoke with one teacher who assigned her students to write an extended response to a question. When she graded it, however, the items that were allocated the most points were neatness and spelling. Whether or not the student actually answered the question and provided evidence for the response were small portions of the grade. This isn't fair to students. You can count those items, but the main focus of your grade should be whether or not it meets the standards, goals, and objectives.

Don't Count Effort, Behavior, or Attendance

One of the mistakes I made as a teacher was grading on things that didn't involve the actual work. For example, if a student "tried hard," I gave credit for effort. So as long as they attempted to do the work, students received partial credit, whether any of it was correct. I've since learned to give students multiple opportunities to complete the work correctly, along with coaching the student, but effort alone does not qualify for a high grade.

Next, I unconsciously graded based on behavior. It wasn't that blatant, of course, but if I had a student who was well-behaved, and there was a questionable call on the grade, I gave the student the benefit of the doubt. I should have graded equally, no matter what a student's behavior was. But I was young, and didn't realize I was doing it.

Finally, it's easy to incorporate attendance into grading. If a student was absent, I'd take points off for each day he or she was late with the assignment. It didn't matter why they were absent; my policy demanded points taken off for late work. In effect, I penalized students because they weren't at school. Some had good reasons for missing, some less so. But the bottom line was that I was choosing to grade, not on their work, but on their presence.

If I could return to my classroom and do it again, I would remove these three factors from grading. A grade should reflect the quality of work, not anything else.

Involve Students in Grading

Students feel more ownership when they are involved in the grading process. So, involve them in the grading process. Be sure they understand what the grade represents, have them look at samples and grade the items themselves, ask them to self-assess their work, and let them create rubrics. In one classroom, the students determined the levels for rubrics.

Student-Created Categories

4 . . . overachiever
3 . . . proficient-got it
2 . . . stuck in the middle
1 . . . at the bottom

As the teacher explained, "I didn't particularly like the names for some of the levels, but the students chose them, so I stayed with them."

After students create the levels, guide them through the process of what would be an "A", or "B", etc. Student ownership doesn't mean you aren't involved; it simply means you guide the process rather than doing it all yourself. After the rubric is finished, ask students to assess a sample paper so they see how the rubric applies to actual work. Then, revise it together, and you can move forward with its use. It's an excellent way for students to be invested in grading.

Never Give Zeroes

Too often, students don't complete work that requires a demonstration of learning. Typically, this results in a low grade. We often think this means students learn the importance of responsibility, but more often they learn that if they are willing to "take a lower grade or a zero," then they do not actually have to complete their work. For some, that is a preferable alternative to doing work. Perhaps they don't fully understand the assignment or they may not want to complete it. However, if we truly have high expectations for students, we don't let them off the hook for learning. The Southern Regional Education Board promoted a policy of no zeroes as an Instant Credit Recovery Model.

Eight Key Elements of the Instant Credit Recovery Model

- Teachers no longer assign grades below a C.
- Eliminate the use of zeroes.
- Late work is late, but it must be completed if teachers are to correctly determine if students know, understand, and are able to do whatever the verb within the standard calls for.
- Students must be given extra help opportunities (required) to learn the information, skill, or concept to complete assignments.
- Students must retake tests that they fail and redo all assignments they earn less than a C grade on.
- Consequences change for students not having work ready to turn in on time.
- Grading systems change from zeroes or failing grades to "I's" or some other form of non-grade.
- A few students will still fail no matter what. The goal is to get MORE students to complete MORE assignments and assessments to the proficient level of the standard.

The use of a "Credit Recovery," "Not Yet," or "Incomplete" policy for projects and assignments shifts the emphasis to learning and allows students to revise and resubmit work until it is at an acceptable level. This is far more rigorous than allowing students to not learn. Requiring quality work, work that meets the teacher's expectations, lets students know that the priority is learning, not simple completion of an assignment.

Grade for Quality, not Completion

Also, be sure that your grade reflects the quality of the work, not just completion or the quantity of included items. I received a copy of an assignment for a tenth-grade honors course. Students had a week to complete the project. Take a look.

History Project #1 _____ Due: (one week) _____

Wanted Poster

We have studied several individuals who made significant contributions during the Renaissance and Reformation. You will create a wanted poster about one of these people. The information on the poster must include:

1. Poster **MUST** be on an 8½ × 11 sheet of paper.   **(10 points)**
2. Mug shot—We need to know what they look like!   **(10 points)**
3. First and Last name of your historical figure.   **(5 points)**
4. Birth date and year of death.   **(5 points)**
5. What country were they born in **and** where did they do their work?   **(10 points)**
6. What are they famous (wanted) for? 5–8 complete sentences, in your own words, for full credit.   **(30 points)**
7. A fact that you found interesting **OR** a quote by the person.   **(10 points)**
8. Print out or photocopy of your sources with info highlighted.   **(15 points)**
9. Your name on the bottom right corner.   **(5 points)**

There are several ways to increase the rigor of this assignment. Additionally, rather than students earning credit for completion, as it was originally created, scoring should be based on quality.

Revision of Grading for Wanted Poster

Percentage of Grade	Requirements
20%	Connections: Narrative includes key life events, family, possible associates, other locations visited or other places the person lived to help with locating the person.
25%	Synthesis based on multiple sources (minimum of 5): Information in paper is synthesized and confirmed from multiple sources, rather than summarized from an isolated source. It is also cited appropriately to demonstrate synthesis.
25%	Analysis: As a conclusion, narrative includes an analysis of the individual, including strengths, weaknesses, and possible other contributions the person could have made to the movement. Although your opinion, analysis should be based on the information gathered.
20%	Written narrative: Overall flow and quality of writing, appropriate information included, extraneous information excluded. Quotes and other information support key points made throughout the paper.
10%	Basic requirements: Completion of all aspects of assignment, 8" x 10" paper, "mug shot," your name at the bottom right corner, reference list in appropriate format on reference page, word-processed narrative with 12-point font and 1-inch margins, minimum of 5 sources, and photocopy of sources with information highlighted.

THINK ABOUT IT!

How effective is your grading according to these criteria?
Which is your strength? Which would you like to improve?

Other Aspects of Grading

Extra Credit

When I was teaching, I struggled with the whole concept of extra credit. It never seemed to accomplish what I thought it would. The students who usually earned it, didn't really need it, earning an A plus instead of an A or an A instead of a B. It also seemed to overemphasize points vs. learning.

Several years ago, one of my graduate students was furious because I wouldn't give her extra credit. She was on the borderline between an A and a B, and she wanted me to increase one low grade because she had done a good job "the rest of the time." In effect, she wanted me to give her extra credit on a very poor assignment because she wanted it.

I considered this request, as well as how a similar situation would conclude in real life. If my husband does extra work on a project for his job, he doesn't get an extra boost in his salary. It may impact his future salary or any raises, but he doesn't get an additional payment for his quality work. On the other hand, if he did a poor job on the project, he certainly doesn't get rewarded for doing something else to make up for it. In other words, extra credit isn't a part of the real world.

Assessing Group Work

How should you assess group work? Some researchers recommend that you not assign group grades, as it doesn't meet the purpose of grading: to reflect each student's learning of an objective. With group work, you could have two students who learn the same amount but receive different grades because they are in two different groups. How is that rigorous?

What is the solution? Susan Brookhart, in *Grading and Group Work: How Do I Assess Individual Learning When Students Work Together?* provides four steps we can follow when assessing cooperative learning.

Steps for Assessing Cooperative Learning

1. Ask yourself what it is you want students to learn by engaging in the group project. The answer should relate to one or more state standards or curricular goals.
2. Define precisely the knowledge and skills that students need to be able to complete the group project. The project should tap both learning and process skills, and content knowledge and skills. List

---

them separately. If no learning and process skills are required, then the project isn't an effective use of group work. If no content knowledge and skills are required, then the project isn't an effective use of instructional and assessment time.

3. Plan ways to observe and assess (but not grade) the learning and process skills—both individual and collective—and to give feedback about them.

4. Plan ways to observe and assess individuals' content knowledge and skills. These assessments can be graded.

Notice she isn't saying not to use group work. Rather, choose when and how you use it, and always grade individually.

THINK ABOUT IT!

How do you currently assess group work?
Is there something you would like to change?

Homework

Homework is a part of most of today's classrooms. One of the myths about rigor is that increased homework is rigorous. That's not true. It's the quality of homework not the quantity that makes a difference.

We typically assign homework in order to extend learning beyond the classroom. Sometimes we think we just don't have enough time to complete everything during class, so we use homework to gain additional times. Other times, we give homework because we believe it teaches responsibility. And, at times, we assign homework because parents expect us to.

What does this mean to us? Homework can be effective, but we must plan for its use. Cathy Vatterott, in her book *Rethinking Homework: Best Practices that Support Diverse Needs*, provides some guiding principles as we plan for homework.

Principles for Assigning Homework

- Homework should be clearly connected to student learning.
- Skills require practice.
- More time on task enhances learning.
- The quality is as important as the amount of time needed to complete the work.
- Children differ in motivation, persistence, and organizational skills and this impacts homework.
- Frustration is detrimental to motivation and desire to learn.

An important action for teachers is to set the purpose of homework for students. Cathy suggests sample statements to use with younger and older students.

Sample Statements on the Purpose of Homework

Younger Students	Older Students
The reason for today's homework is . . .	The reason for today's homework is to . . .
• so you can practice doing something you learned in school. • so I can find out if you understand what you learned today. • to show you something we will learn about soon.	• allow you to apply something you have already learned to a new situation. • allow you to pull together several things you have already learned. • allow you to analyze something you have already learned.

Communicating Results

Finally, communicating results to students and families is an important aspect of grading. As you are asking students to move to more rigorous levels of work, communicating progress is critical. There are two major ways to communicate results: report cards and student-led conferences.

Report Cards

Report cards are the main way teachers communicate results of assessments to parents, families, and students. Report cards typically provide space for a grade, but you should add comments whenever possible. Comments are more helpful because they provide specific feedback as to strengths and challenges.

What makes an effective report card? Carol Ann Tomlinson and Tonya Moon share nine principles for effective grading. They are particularly pertinent to report cards.

Nine Guiding Principles

1. Base grades on clearly specified learning goals.
2. Use grades that are criterion-based, not comparative.
3. Don't over-grade student work.
4. Use only quality assessments.
5. Reduce "grade fog" (things that muddle the meaning or clarity of the grade).
6. Eliminate "mathematical grade fog" (giving zeroes, which artificially deflate grades; averaging grades, which overemphasizes outlier scores).
7. Grade more heavily later in the grading cycle rather than earlier.
8. Use 3P grading (report several grades each for student's performance or product, the student's process, and the student's progress).
9. Involve students in the assessment and grading process.

Student-Led Conferences

A second strategy for communicating results is student-led conferences. They have risen in popularity in recent years, and reflect a more rigorous way to communicate because students must take a leadership role. Teachers participate, but they move into the role of a facilitator. What does a student-led conference look like?

Structure for Student-Led Conference

- Welcome your guests (family members).
- Introduce your teacher.
- Share your goals (should be written).
- Show your chart that demonstrates progress.
- Show examples of your work that is reflected on the chart.
- Ask if your guests have any questions.
- Ask if your teacher has anything to add.
- Complete the summary sheet together.

Sample Summary Sheet	
Goals:	
Things I Do Well	Things I'm Working On

You'll also want to guide parents as to the types of questions to ask. Remember, this is typically new for them.

Sample Questions for Parents to Ask

- What are you most proud of?
- What have you learned?
- What are you still working on?
- What did you struggle with?
- Did you reach your goals?
- Questions I have for the teacher as my child presents.

THINK ABOUT IT!

How do you currently communicate results to students and parents/families? Is there a way you could improve that communication?

Conclusion

Grading is one of the most challenging aspects of assessment in a rigorous classroom. The purposes of grading provide a framework for our grading practices. Then, characteristics of effective grading such as the use of rubrics and aligning grading to standards inform our practice. Finally, other aspects of grading such as assessing group work and communicating grades are important aspects that enhance our grading processes.

9

The Critical Role of Feedback in the Rigorous Classroom

Feedback is a critical part of a rigorous classroom. If rigor is about students learning at higher levels, feedback is the staircase that allows the step-by-step growth to happen. John Hattie lists feedback as one of the top actions that positively impact teaching and learning. In this chapter, we'll look at the relationship between motivation and feedback and the characteristics of effective feedback, we'll discuss two types of feedback, and finally, we'll consider peer feedback, and feedback in self-assessment.

Motivation and Feedback

In a rigorous classroom, the teacher incorporates motivational elements throughout instruction and assessment. Although all assessment is related to student motivation, feedback has a special relationship, since feedback is personal. Student motivation consists of two factors: value and success. Students are more motivated when they see value in what they are doing and when they feel successful. Both are impacted by feedback.

First, students need to see the value in feedback. If it is vague or not relevant to them they will simply tune it out. That's why we need to make sure our feedback is closely tied to what we have asked the students to do. Hopefully, when we assigned the work, we incorporated real-life connections. This will then make the feedback useful.

Second, motivated students feel successful. The most effective feedback helps students see what they have done well, so they can feel successful; then it assists in showing the student what he or she can do to be even more successful. It's important to pay attention to both of these facets of student motivation as you provide feedback to your students. Think of them as the building blocks or foundation for your work.

Characteristics of Effective Feedback

What does effective feedback look like? It's important to consider because feedback can have a negative effect on students. For example, if the only feedback is whether a question is right or wrong, no additional learning occurs. How can we expect students to work at a rigorous level it we don't provide the best possible feedback?

Characteristics of Effective Feedback

- Related to Goals
- Timely
- Frequent
- Specific, Clear, and Accurate
- Formative
- Progress-Oriented
- Focuses on Next Steps
- Provides Explanations
- Emphasizes Learning, not Personality
- Uses Visual Representations

Related to Goals

First, effective feedback is related to goals, objectives, and standards. This sounds basic, but too often, we focus our feedback on other, possibly important items. I observed a teacher whose students completed an analysis of a science experiment, a rigorous task. The goal was clear in terms of analysis and was focused on what the students learned from the experiment and other possible outcomes based on differing variables. When providing written feedback, the first-year teacher wrote most of her comments about the group work and the role each student played. While important, it was not part of the assignment, and did not relate to the stated objective. It distracted students from the task at hand.

Timely

Effective feedback is also timely. It is given after initial instruction, so that students have an opportunity to be successful. It is also provided soon after students have completed their work. If you wait too long, students tend to forget what they have done, and the feedback is meaningless.

Tips for Providing Efficient Feedback

- Check for completion, with some comments
- Keep a list of common feedback statements as a reference
- Use rubrics
- Use peer feedback

Frequent

Next, feedback should be frequent. The question is, how frequent? I wish I could give you a formula, but there simply isn't one. Sometimes, you will give individual students feedback every day, or even multiple times a day in an elementary classroom. Other times, if you are giving feedback on 150 assignments, it may be once a week. I think the most effective guideline is that feedback should be a regular part of your classroom, and it should be considered in a broad sense. For example, there is verbal feedback as you monitor the class, peer feedback when students are working with a partner or with a small group, self-reflective feedback when students are assessing themselves, and more formal written feedback. Because you are increasing the rigor of your classroom, you want to be sure to incorporate ample feedback so students can understand where they stand.

Specific, Clear, and Accurate

Feedback should also be specific, clear, and accurate. Specificity and clarity are critical; without it, students do not have a clear picture as to what they can and cannot do. For example, simply telling students, "You did a good job with your writing. Keep it up." isn't helpful. The student doesn't understand what he or she did to make the writing "good," so he or she doesn't know what to do next time.

Formative

Effective feedback is formative, rather than summative. Feedback should help students know how to improve for the future. If it is used in a summative manner, it's too late for students to improve.

Progress-Oriented

As a formative assessment, feedback should focus on progress. Again, feedback should help students move forward. When I was a teacher, sometimes I told students what they did wrong, but I didn't help them understand how to make progress, which leads to our next characteristic.

Focuses on Next Steps

To help students make progress, you'll need to show them the next step they should take. A teacher in one of my workshops said, "Once I tell them what they didn't do right, they should know what to do next." My response? If students knew what to do, they would do it. If their work needs improvement, they need your help, and just telling them to improve isn't enough.

Provides Explanations

Feedback that is effective expands on comments to provide an explanation. Let's say you have a student working on a math problem in which the student answered with a positive number rather than a negative number. You might tell him or her first to "Review the steps in the problem." A deeper explanation would include guiding him or her to remember the rules for adding and subtracting positive and negative integers, and asking him or her to explain the steps he or she followed for adding or subtracting to answer the question.

Emphasizes Learning, not Personality

Effective feedback also emphasizes the learning of the student. When a student hears feedback that is personal (as opposed to personalized), they don't know what to do with it. If a teacher tells me that I am so smart, what does that tell me about my learning?

Making Feedback Learning-Focused, Not Personal	
Learning-Focused Feedback	*Personality-Focused Feedback*
When you did this, it added to the explanation.	Fantastic!
You did these particular things well.	You did well today.
I noticed that you did this. Why did you do that? How might you do it differently?	You are so smart.

Uses Visual Representations

Finally, using visual representations enhances the effectiveness of your feedback. I was surprised to learn this when I first read it, but then I considered what happened with my students. One year, we kept a log of their strengths and weaknesses for each assignment, so they could see their progress and also identify patterns. Students responded well, and seemed to learn more throughout the year. Verbal feedback is certainly appropriate, but providing written feedback, as well as charts or graphs to show growth is more effective.

THINK ABOUT IT!

Which of these characteristics is your strongest in terms of feedback? Which do you think you could improve upon?

Types of Feedback

There are two types of feedback to use with students.

Types of Feedback

- Feedback on what you learn
- Feedback on how you learn

First, there is feedback on what you learn. This focuses on content mastery. What specific skills have been mastered and which ones need more instruction? This is particularly important in a rigorous classroom, as you are asking students to work at increasingly more challenging levels. In addition to assessing the actual work, a useful tool is a simple form for students to summarize their understanding.

Sample Content Mastery Form	
I definitely understand . . .	
I am still trying to figure out . . .	
I don't understand . . .	

Next, there is feedback on how you learn. In this case, you want to help students understand their learning, and be able to apply their learning to different experiences. You will want to provide feedback to students about their learning process based on your own observations. The researchers at Mindset Works (www.mindsetworks.com) created a set of feedback prompts related to growth mindset (see next page). They are excellent for helping students focus on how they learn.

THINK ABOUT IT!

Have you used feedback on "how you learn?" How could you incorporate that more into your instruction?

Growth Mindset Feedback

*As students begin to work on their learning objectives, growth-minded language guides and motivates them to ensure that they remain **persistent, resilient, and focused** on the process of learning. It is important to give learners feedback about their progress and their results so they can specifically see their growth.*

Use these language frames when interacting with your students in the following situations.

When they struggle despite strong effort

- OK, so you didn't do as well as you wanted to. Let's look at this as an opportunity to learn.
- What did you do to prepare for this? Is there anything you could do to prepare differently next time?
- You are not there/here **yet**.
- When you think you can't do it, remind yourself that you can't do it **yet.**
- I expect you to make some mistakes. It is the <u>kinds</u> of mistakes that you make along the way that tell me how to support you.
- Mistakes are welcome here!
- You might be struggling, but you are making progress. I can see your growth (in these places.)
- Look at how much progress you made on this. Do you remember how much more challenging this was (yesterday/last week/last year?)
- Of course it's tough—school is here to makes our brains stronger!
- If it were easy, you wouldn't be learning anything!
- You can do it—it's tough, but you can; let's break it down into steps.
- Let's stop here and return tomorrow with a fresher brain.
- I admire your persistence and I appreciate your hard work. It will pay off.

When they struggle and need help with strategies

- Let's think about how to improve (the accuracy of) this section/paragraph/sentence/word choice/logic/description/problem/calculation.
- Let me add new information to help you solve this....
- Here are some strategies to figure this out.
- Describe your process for completing this task.
- Let's do one together, out loud.
- Let's practice (skill) so we can move it from our short-term to our long-term memory.
- Just try—we can always fix mistakes once I see where you are getting held up.
- Let me explain in another way with different words.
- What parts were difficult for you? Let's look at them.
- Let's ask _____ for advice—s/he may be able to explain/suggest some ideas/recommend some strategies.
- Let's write a plan for practicing and/or learning.
- If you make_____changes, we can reassess your score. Let's discuss a plan for you.

www.mindsetworks.com/websitemedia/resources/growth-mindset-feedback-tool.pdf. Used with permission.

continued

When they are making progress

- Hey that's a tough problem/task/concept that you've been working on for a while. What strategies are you using?
- I can see a difference in this work compared to_____. You have really grown (in these areas.)
- I see you using your strategies/tools/notes/etc. Keep it up!
- Hey! You were working on this for awhile and you didn't quit!
- Your hard work is clearly evident in your process/project/essay/assignment.

When they succeed with strong effort

- I am so proud of the effort you put forth to/in/with_____.
- I am very proud of you for not giving up, and look what you have to show for it!
- Congratulations—you really used great strategies for studying, managing your time (behavior, etc..)
- I want you to remember for a moment how challenging this was when you began. Look at how far you have come!
- All that hard work and effort paid off!
- The next time you have a challenge like this, what will you do?
- What choices did you make that you think contributed to your success?
- It's exciting to see the difference in your work now when I compare it to your earlier work.
- I can see you really enjoyed learning_____.

When they succeed easily without effort

- It's great that you have that down. Now we need to find something a bit more challenging so you can grow.
- It looks like your skills weren't really challenged by this assignment. Sorry for wasting your time!
- I don't want you to be bored because you're not challenging yourself.
- We need to raise the bar for you now.
- You're ready for something more difficult.
- What skill would you like to work on next?
- What topic would you like to learn more about next?

www.mindsetworks.com/websitemedia/resources/growth-mindset-feedback-tool.pdf.
Used with permission.

Peer Feedback

Not all feedback needs to come from you. One alternative is the use of peer feedback. Although not something you might use every day, you can build it in as a regular part of your assessment plan. As a bonus, shifting ownership to students allows them to demonstrate a higher level of understanding, which is a critical part of a rigorous classroom. However, as students learn how to give feedback to each other, you will need to provide some structure.

Sample Peer Feedback Form	
One Thing I Like . . .	
One Thing You Could Improve . . .	
One More Thing I Like . . .	

Student Name _____

Conference Date _____

Grows

_____

_____

_____

_____

_____

Glows!

_____

_____

_____

_____

_____

Grows and Glows

Grows and Glows

In some cases, you will want to be more specific in terms of what students should look for in another student's work.

Excerpt of Peer Feedback Form for Writing (Middle/High School)			
	Not There	*Tried*	*On Target*
Has strong thesis			
Provides ample supporting details			
Interesting and varied content-specific vocabulary is used			
Does the conclusion make a strong argument based on the thesis and details and call for action by the reader?			

THINK ABOUT IT!

How do you use peer feedback in your classroom?
What would you like to try during the next several weeks?

Self-Assessment and Feedback

Asking students to assess themselves and provide feedback both to themselves and to you is also important. For higher levels of rigor, students need to reflect on their own learning and determine what they know, what they don't know, and possible next steps. We've looked at examples of self-reflection in Chapters 3 and 4, but let's add a few more to our teaching toolkit since it's such an important part of the feedback process.

You may want students to simply assess themselves in terms of their level of knowledge. In Laundry Day, students group themselves in the four categories shown below (named after detergents). With the groupings, you can then determine how much reteaching needs to occur.

Laundry Day	
Category	*Student's Perspective*
Tide	I'm drowning in information.
Gain	I understand the basics, but I'm missing a few parts.
Bold	I'm confident, but I'm missing some details.
Cheer	I'm sure I understand, so I'm looking for something new.

A teacher in one of my workshops shared a similar strategy. Her version was "Which Road Are You On?"

Which Road Are You On?	
Category	*Student's Perspective*
The Dirt Road	There's so much dust, I can't see where I'm going! Help!!
The Paved Road	It's fairly smooth, but there are many potholes along the way.
The Highway	I feel fairly confident but have an occasional need to slow down.
The Interstate	I'm traveling along and could easily give directions to someone else.

As an alternative, you may want more information from your students. In the first example, you simply provide open-ended statements.

Open-Ended Statements

This was great!	I was surprised when...
I'd like to do this next...	One question I have is...

For a more formal option, Peter Pappas provides questions along the levels of Bloom's Taxonomy. This is ideal for older students.

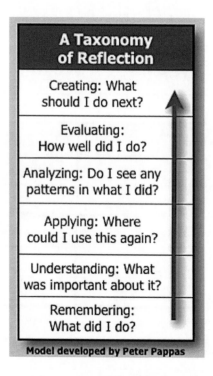

A Taxonomy of Reflection

Reprinted with permission from www.peterpappas.com/2010/01/reflective-student-taxonomy-reflection.html.

As a third choice, Christy Matkovich and Lindsey Grant created a math processing chart (see next page), which can be used when tests are returned to students.

THINK ABOUT IT!

Which of these strategies would you like to try with your students?

Understanding Math Better

Name _____ Date _____

Math Test _____ Teacher _____

Question:

My original answer:

My new solution (you must show your work, including all steps):

The correct answer:

Why I missed the question on the original test (circle one):

       I didn't understand the question.

       I thought I had it right.

       I skipped a step.

       I studied this but I forgot.

       I had no clue about this.

       I ran out of time or guessed.

       I made a careless mistake.

Why I know I have the right answer now:

Conclusion

Feedback is an important part of a rigorous classroom; it allows students to grow to their full potential. However, it must be effective. This means including timeliness, frequency, specificity, and a focus on growth. It's also important to consider the types of feedback, as well as incorporating feedback from peers and from the students themselves. Taking all of these into consideration will strengthen your assessment.

10

Working Together to Improve Assessment in Rigorous Classrooms

As we finish our journey together, let's turn our attention to working together to improve assessment. So far, we've targeted the nuts and bolts of what you can do to enhance rigor and assessment in your classroom. In this chapter, we'll focus on working with other teachers to further enrich your work. Working with other teachers can be challenging, but it can also be very beneficial. We're going to discuss ways to make it positive.

Benefits of Collaboration

Collaboration has several benefits, both for teachers and students. First, anytime teachers meet together for a reflective discussion of learning, everyone leaves with a new understanding. There is value in sharing differing opinions. We learn when we all share our points of view and talk about them. When we work together, not only do we accomplish more, we are all lifted to a higher level of thinking. Positive collaboration elevates each individual.

Collaboration also enhances our self-confidence. When I was a new teacher, I second-guessed myself fairly often. I was unsure if what I was doing was best for my students; not just good enough. However, when I shared my thoughts with other teachers, and we discussed possible adjustments, I was able to improve. Although I didn't take every suggestion, their perspectives helped me be more confident.

Building on that, collaborating enhances consistency. I don't know about where you live, but in my experience, when parents are together—either at the ball field or the grocery store—they compare what teachers are doing. I have found that if one teacher is grading differently from others, it can cause problems. You don't want to be challenged by parents who think you "grade too hard." It's far easier to defend a decision on assessments, whether it is the amount of work assigned or the grading, when multiple teachers are on the same page.

Second, your grading and feedback are more effective. Once again, because of your collaborative conversations, you have a better idea of specific criteria that makes a "good" response. That means you can then give better feedback and more accurate grades to your students, who also benefit.

Collaborative Norms

In any collaborative process, it's important to have agreed upon norms. Without them, the process can deteriorate into personal attacks, or an off task discussion. Robert Garmston and Bruce Wellman (www.adaptiveschools. com) have created a set of seven norms of collaboration. I think you will find them helpful as you work together.

Seven Norms of Collaboration for Productive Communication

1. Pausing
2. Paraphrasing
3. Posing Questions
4. Putting Ideas on the Table
5. Providing Data
6. Paying Attention to Self and Others
7. Presuming Positive Intentions

THINK ABOUT IT!

How will these norms help you and your fellow teachers collaborate?

Overall Process for Collaboration

Next, we're going to look at four specific strategies for collaborating to increase the rigor of your assessments. However, let's quickly put those strategies in the context of the overall process of collaboration. By following these ten steps, you are more likely to accomplish your overall goal: to improve student learning at a rigorous level.

---

10 Step Process for Collaboration

1. Gain commitment from teachers.
2. Garner support from leadership.
3. Agree upon the purpose.
4. Identify desired outcomes.
5. Follow a strategy for sharing (next in the chapter).
6. Evaluate what you've learned.
7. Make decisions based upon your data.
8. Plan your next steps.
9. Implement your planned actions.
10. Revisit and make needed adjustments.

There are four strategies for sharing work (step 5 in the process) to increase the rigor of your assignments and assessments.

Four Strategies

- Matching Assessments to Goals
- Assessing the Assignment's Rigor
- Assessing Expectations with Vertical Alignment
- Assessing Student Work

Matching Assessments to Goals

The first way to collaborate to increase the rigor of your assessments is to check the alignment of goals and objectives to your assessments (see Chapter 2 for more on goals and objectives). You would be surprised at how often assessments don't match. For example, students are given an essay question and asked to define inflation and compare it to deflation. However, the objective is to give a description of inflation and compare it to deflation, explaining the impact on the economy. Notice that at first glance, the assessment matches the desired outcome. It addresses the topic. But when we analyze the specific objective, it's clear that this particular assessment only scratches the surface. Although it asked them to compare inflation and deflation, it does not address the effect on the economy. A more aligned assignment would be an essay question which asks students to describe the similarities and differences between inflation and deflation, as well as the impact they have on the economy, including at least three examples with supporting evidence.

Assessing the Assignment's Rigor

A second collaborative activity is to measure whether your assignments are rigorous. There is an appropriate time for less rigorous assessments, especially as you are scaffolding learning. However, too often we stay at these lower levels, so it's important to ensure that the majority of your assessments are rigorous.

There are a variety of ways to determine the rigor of your assessment. It's important to use a standard to help you determine what is rigorous. We'll look at two; choose the one that best fits your needs.

Two Measures of Rigor

- Bloom's Taxonomy
- Webb's *Depth of Knowledge*

Bloom's Taxonomy

Probably the most popular tool used to determine rigor is Bloom's Taxonomy.

Levels of Bloom's Taxonomy

- Remember
- Understand
- Apply
- Analyze
- Evaluate
- Create

I think Bloom's is a good starting point, but I also find a challenge with this approach. We have come to associate Bloom's levels with specific verbs. However, verbs can be deceptive. For example, on the taxonomy, *create* is at the highest level. But is that always true? When conducting walkthroughs in a school, I observed a lesson in which students were creating get-well cards for a sick classmate. Is that rigorous? Of course not. The verb is deceptive. Let's look at another example.

> After studying Greek and Roman civilizations, students, create a 3-dimensional model to compare and contrast the two civilizations using only edible material.

Is that assignment rigorous? Students are asked to design a creative way to present their information. It seems challenging. After all, they have to be creative to complete the project. But if we take away the creative aspect, students are basically recalling information, which is at a low level of Bloom's. I believe we should provide opportunities for students to demonstrate their creative side, but don't let that be an excuse for rigor.

Webb's Depth of Knowledge (DOK)

I prefer using Webb's *Depth of Knowledge* as a benchmark of rigor. Webb's DOK has four levels, focusing on depth and complexity.

> ### Webb's *Depth of Knowledge*
>
> **Level One**: Recall
> **Level Two**: Skill/Concept
> **Level Three**: Strategic Thinking
> **Level Four**: Extended Thinking

As a side note, there is a very popular circle diagram of DOK on the Internet. It is a circle, divided into quarters; and each section lists verbs for the level. However, simplifying the DOK to verbs takes us back to the same problem as with Bloom's. Verbs can be deceptive.

When writing another of my books, *Rigor in Your Classroom: A Toolkit for Teachers*, I contacted Dr. Webb's office to ask to reprint the wheel in my book. I received a quick and clear response. Dr. Webb did not create the DOK verb wheel, he does not endorse it, nor does he believe it represents the four dimensions. I understand why. The *Depth of Knowledge* levels are descriptors of depth and complexity that go far beyond simplistic verbs.

For example, take a look at the full description of the four levels for English Language Arts on the next page.

Do you see the deeper structure? It's more comprehensive, which provides a strong gauge of the rigor of an assignment. Notice that although Levels One and Two are important, Levels Three and Four are considered rigorous.

With your colleagues, choose an assessment you are currently using. Compare it to the criteria we discussed. How did your assessment match up? If you answered yes to a majority of the questions, then your assessment is at Level Two of Webb's *Depth of Knowledge*. That doesn't mean it's a bad assessment, but it's not rigorous (Levels Three and Four). You would want to increase the level of rigor in the current assignment.

THINK ABOUT IT!

Which of the models for assessing work samples would you like to try?

Assessing Expectations with Vertical Alignment

Building on the first two strategies, we'll now turn our attention to checking the teachers vertical alignment of assessments. For this, you will be working with teachers across grade levels. Choose a general topic, such as landforms, forms of government, integers, or expository writing. Ask each teacher to bring a sample assignment from his or her grade level.

Next, look at the goals and objectives for each assessment. Ideally, the goals and objectives form a staircase, moving up in incremental stages. If your assignments don't do this, you can still use this activity, but in a future discussion, try to find goals and objectives that follow this format.

Then, begin to compare the assessments. Follow the steps on p. 128 as you evaluate the variety of assessments.

Summary Definitions of *Depth of Knowledge* (DOK) for English Language Arts

LEVEL 1	LEVEL 2	LEVEL 3	LEVEL 4
Requires students to recall, observe, question, or represent facts, simple skills, or abilities. Requires only surface understanding of text, often verbatim recall. *Examples:* • Support ideas by reference to verbatim (or only slightly paraphrased) details in text. • Use a dictionary to find meanings of words. • Recognize figurative language in a passage. • Identify correct spelling or meaning of words.	Requires processing beyond recall and observation. Requires both comprehension and subsequent processing of text or portions of text. Involves ordering, classifying text as well as identifying patterns, relationships, and main points. *Examples:* • Use context to identify unfamiliar words. • Predict a logical outcome. • Identify and summarize main points. • Apply knowledge of conventions of standard American English. • Compose accurate summaries of the major events in a narrative.	Requires students to go beyond text. Requires students to explain, generalize, and connect ideas. Involves deep inferencing, prediction, elaboration, and summary. Requires students to support positions using prior knowledge and evidence and to manipulate themes across passages. *Examples:* • Determine effect of author's purpose on text elements. • Critically analyze literature. • Compose focused, organized, coherent, purposeful prose. • Evaluate the internal logic or credibility of a message.	Requires complexity at least at the level of DOK 3 but also an extended time to complete the task, such as conducting a research project over many weeks. A project that requires extended time but repetitive or lower-DOK tasks is not at Level 4. May require hypotheses and performing complex analyses and connections among texts. *Examples:* • Analyzing and synthesizing information from multiple sources. • Examine and explain alternative perspectives across sources. • Describe and illustrate common themes across a variety of texts. • Create compositions that synthesize, analyze, and evaluate.

Assessing for Increased Rigor Across Grade Levels

1. Begin with the lowest grade level.
2. Does the assessment match the goal and/or objective?
3. Is the assignment rigorous (use strategies described earlier in this chapter)?
4. Complete this process for each assignment in the various grade levels.
5. Compare the two lowest grade level assignments.
6. Do you see an increase in the level of rigor?
    *   Questions build on prior knowledge from earlier grade levels.
    *   Questions move beyond reviewing content.
    *   Assignment shows a clear progression of challenge.
7. Continue to compare, moving up one grade level at a time.

Finally, discuss any revisions needed. I was working with a school a few years ago. The fifth-grade teachers were using a basic assessment on summarizing information. The assignment itself was not that rigorous; students had been taught to summarize in earlier grades. Certainly, the students needed some review, but the teacher was not moving beyond the simplistic summary paragraphs. The next day, I was in the high school, visiting a science classroom. Students were summarizing the experiment they had completed. They were not analyzing, evaluating, or providing evidence; they were simply summarizing—the exact skill from the fifth-grade class. When I discussed what I had seen in the elementary school with the high school teacher, he was surprised. He said the students didn't know how to write summaries, so he was teaching them how. He had no idea it was being taught at lower levels. His students had told him they had not learned how to write a summary.

One thing I learned as a teacher was that students always say that. After teaching seventh grade one year, I was moved to the eighth grade. I had about 20% of the same students. Oftentimes, they acted as if they had never seen the material I was using for a quick review. I learned to use assessments that focused on new application of the information, especially when reviewing concepts from a previous year. I also reviewed content in the context of current goals and objectives, so students were required to make connections.

Let me reinforce why vertical alignment of assessments is so important. Assessments reflect your instruction. Several years ago, I visited a middle school. One of my favorite activities while visiting is to ask student, "If you were in charge of the school, what would you change?" One student, Gabrielle, surprised me with her answer.

"If I was in charge, for students who are in lower-level classes, I'd put them in higher-level classes. If you don't know much, you shouldn't teach them to not know much over and over again."

Apply her response to assessments. Can you imagine students feeling similarly? Students can become bored because we're assessing the same thing over and over again, and usually in the same way.

Assessing Student Work

Now, we're going to turn our attention from assessing the assessments to assessing the students' work. I saw an excellent example of the process we'll look at in Cleveland County, North Carolina. As they described the process, which I have modified, I immediately saw the value. I'll describe it from a school-based perspective, and then share some additional steps to apply the process on a district-wide basis. To do this, you'll want to work across a grade level in specific subject areas.

First, each teacher should bring an assignment, along with three samples of student work; one that he or she considers to be high quality (an A), one that is average quality (a C), and one of low quality (an F). Remember to bring enough copies for everyone in the group. The initial teacher begins by describing the assignment, and sharing the average sample. Teachers then discuss their opinions as to the quality of the student work.

Discussion Questions

- Do you consider this response to be average?
- What are the specific aspects of the response that make it so? For example, why isn't it above average, why is it higher than a failing response.
- How does it compare to a sample of average work for your students?

Next, another teacher shares his or her average sample, following the same process. Now, compare the two. Are they similar? How so? If not, what makes them different? Continue to add other teachers' samples. As you discuss the samples, keep a chart of examples and non-examples of the characteristics of an "average response."

Now, go back through the process with the high or above average assignments. Then compare those characteristics to the average papers and see if you can add any more to your average chart.

Finally, assess and discuss the below average/unacceptable responses in a similar manner. Then, compare your characteristic charts at each level. Adjust and clarify the characteristics as a group. You'll end up with a chart, or a rubric, of the assignment or type of assignment.

If each teacher brings different products (for example, an essay, PowerPoint presentation, or video), you can follow this process. However, you may want to also use a common assessment for a more focused discussion. Your goal is to agree upon "what good looks like" for assessments that are more consistent and reliable, but it is also helpful if you've ever had a conversation with a parent who says, "You graded too hard. My neighbor's daughter did the same thing and she received an A." I'm not saying you can't work independently, or that your judgment isn't on target, but you can learn from working with other teachers and build a deeper understanding of what constitutes quality work.

This process is easily adapted to a district level. You can jump in just as I described, but I recommend school-based comparisons first, and then each school brings three levels of assignments, as well as their charts. This streamlines the district process.

If you noticed, while comparing student work samples, you ultimately created a simple rubric. You can flesh that out to be a collaborative scoring guide, which can be task specific or more generic. In addition to ensuring more consistency across class levels, it's a great professional development tool for new teachers.

THINK ABOUT IT!

Have you worked with other teachers to assess student work? What would be the benefits of doing so?

Conclusion

You can start with any of the strategies I've described. The point is to just start! Working with other teachers will enhance the quality of your assessments, as well as the rigor. As much as we can do on our own, we are always more effective with working in a positive, collaborative environment.

Bibliography

Ainsworth, L., & Viegut, D. (2006). *Common formative assessments: How to connect standards-based instruction and assessment.* Thousand Oaks, CA: Corwin Press.

Barell, J. F. (2016). *Why are school buses always yellow? Teaching for inquiry, K-8.* Thousand Oaks, CA: Corwin Press.

Bartlett, J. (2015). *Outstanding assessment for learning in the classroom.* New York, NY: Routledge.

Black, P., Harrison, C., Lee, C., Marshall, B., & Wiliam D. (2004). *Working inside the black box: Assessment for learning in the classroom, 86, 9–21.*

Blackburn, B. R. (2007). *Classroom instruction from A to Z: How to promote student learning.* New York, NY: Routledge.

Blackburn, B. R. (2008). *Literacy from A to Z: Engaging students in reading, writing, speaking, and listening.* New York, NY: Routledge.

Blackburn, B. R. (2012a). *Rigor made easy.* New York, NY: Routledge.

Blackburn, B. R. (2012b). *Rigor is not a four-letter word* (2nd ed.). New York, NY: Routledge.

Blackburn, B. R. & Witzel, B. (2013). *Rigor for students with special needs.* New York, NY: Routledge.

Blackburn, B. R. (2014). *Rigor in your classroom: A toolkit for teachers.* New York, NY: Routledge.

Blackburn, B. R. (2015). *Motivating struggling learners: 10 ways to build student success.* New York, NY: Routledge.

Brookhart, S. M. (2010). *How to assess higher-order thinking skills in your classroom.* Alexandria, VA: Association for Supervision and Curriculum Development.

Brookhart, S. M. (2011). *Grading and learning: Practices that support student achievement.* Bloomington, IN: Solution Tree Press.

Brookhart, S. (2013). *Grading and group work: How do I assess individual learning when students work together?* Alexandria, VA: Association of Supervision and Curriculum Development.

Brown-Chidsey, R., & Andren, K. J. (2013). *Assessment for intervention: A problem-solving approach.* New York, NY: The Guilford Press.

Burke, K. (2011). *From standards to rubrics in six steps: Tools for assessing student learning* (3rd ed.). Thousand Oaks, CA: Corwin Press.

Butler, S., & McMunn, N. (2006). *A teacher's guide to classroom assessment: Understanding and using assessment to improve student learning.* San Francisco, CA: Jossey-Bass.

Chapman, C., & King, R. (2005). *Differentiated assessment strategies: One tool doesn't fit all.* Thousand Oaks, CA: Corwin Press.

Clarke, S. (2014). *Outstanding formative assessment: Culture and practice.* London: Hodder Education.

Conrad, L. L., Matthews, M., Zimmerman, C., & Allen, P. A. (2008). *Put thinking to the test.* Portland, ME: Stenhouse Publishers.

Cooper, D. (2011). *Redefining fair: How to plan, assess, and grade for excellence in mixed-ability classrooms.* Bloomington, IN: Solution Tree Press.

Costa, A., & Kallick, B. (2008). *Learning and leading with habits of mind: 16 essential characteristics for success.* Alexandria, VA: Association for Supervision and Curriculum Development.

Criswell, J. R. (2006). *Developing assessing literacy: A guide for elementary and middle school teachers.* Norwood, MA: Christopher-Gordon Publishers.

Dean, C. (2012). *Classroom instruction that works research-based strategies for increasing student achievement* (2nd ed.). Alexandria, VA: Association for Supervision and Curriculum Development.

Edutopia. (2016, July 5). *53 ways to check for understanding.* Retrieved July 6, 2016 from www.edutopia.org/resource/checking-understanding-download.

Edutopia. (2016, July 5). *Project rubric.* Retrieved July 6, 2016 from www.edutopia.org/resource/project-rubric-download?utm_source=facebook&utm_medium=post&utm_campaign=resource-project-rubric-download-srn-ss-image.

Ellis, A., & Evans, L. (2010). *Teaching, learning and assessment together: Reflective assessments for middle and high school English and social studies.* Larchmont, NY: Eye on Education.

Fisher, D., & Frey, N. (2007). *Checking for understanding formative assessment techniques for your classroom.* Alexandria, VA: Association for Supervision and Curriculum Development.

Flach, T. (2011). *Engaging students through performance assessment: Creating performance tasks to monitor student learning.* Englewood, CO: Lead Learn Press.

Frey, N., & Fisher, D. (2011). *The formative assessment action plan: Practical steps to more successful teaching and learning.* Alexandria, VA: Association for Supervision and Curriculum Development.

Fuhrken, C. (2012). *What every middle school teacher needs to know about reading tests (from someone who has written them).* Portland, ME: Stenhouse.

Gareis, C. R., & Grant, L. W. (2015). *Teacher-made assessments: How to connect curriculum, instruction, and student learning* (2nd ed.). New York, NY: Routledge.

Greenstein, L. (2010). *What teachers really need to know about formative assessment.* Alexandria, VA: Association for Supervision and Curriculum Development.

Gronlund, G., & James, M. (2013). *Focused observations: How to observe young children for assessment and curriculum planning* (2nd ed.). St. Paul, MN: RedLeaf Press.

Guskey, T. R. (2009). *Practical solutions for serious problems in standards-based grading*. Thousand Oaks, CA: Corwin Press.

Guskey, T. R. (2015). *On your mark: Challenging the conventions of grading and reporting*. Bloomington, IN: Solution Tree Press.

Hattie, J. (2008a). *Visible learning*. New York, NY: Routledge.

Hattie, J. (2008b). *Visible learning for teachers*. New York, NY: Routledge.

Heritage, M., & Stigler, J. (2010). *Formative assessment: Making it happen in the classroom*. Thousand Oaks, CA: Corwin Press.

Hill, D., & Nave, J. (2009). *Power of ICU: The end of student apathy . . . reviving engagement and responsibility*. Maryville, TN: NTLB Publishing.

Jacobs, H. (1997). *Mapping the big picture: Integrating curriculum and assessment, K-12*. Alexandria, VA: Association for Supervision and Curriculum Development.

Johnson, R., & Penny, J. (2009). *Assessing performance: Designing, scoring, and validating performance tasks*. New York, NY: Guilford Press.

Landrigan, C. (2013). *Assessment in perspective: Focusing on the reader behind the numbers*. Portland, ME: Stenhouse.

Lapp, D., Fisher, D., Flood, J., & Cabello, A. (2001). An integrated approach to the teaching and assessment of language arts. In S. R. Hurley & J. V. Tinajero (Eds.), *Literacy assessment of second language learners* (pp. 1–26). Needham Heights, MA: Allyn & Bacon.

Lewin, L., & Shoemaker, B. (2011). *Great performances creating classroom-based assessment tasks* (2nd ed.). Alexandria, VA: Association for Supervision and Curriculum Development.

McTighe, J. & Wiggins, G. (2013). *Essential questions: Opening doors to student understanding*. Alexandria, VA: Association for Supervision and Curriculum Development.

Marzano, R. J. (1988). *Dimensions of thinking*. Alexandria, VA: Association for Supervision and Curriculum Development.

Marzano, R. J. (2007). *Classroom assessment and grading that works*. Alexandria, VA: Association of Supervision and Curriculum Development.

Mayer, R. E., Pintrich, P. R., et al. (Eds.). (2001). *A taxonomy for learning, teaching, and assessing: A revision of Bloom's taxonomy of educational objectives*. New York, NY: Longman.

Moss, C. M., & Brookhart, S. M. (2009). *Advancing formative assessment guide for instructional leaders*. Alexandria, VA: Association for Supervision and Curriculum Development.

Moss, C. M., & Brookhart, S. M. (2012). *Learning targets helping students aim for understanding in today's lesson*. Alexandria, VA: Association for Supervision and Curriculum Development.

Mr Cannon's page. (n.d.). *Teacher resources*. Retrieved July 6, 2016 from http://teachercannon.weebly.com/teacher-resources.html.

National Council of Teachers of English. (1998). *Formative assessment that truly informs instruction*. Retrieved July 6, 2016 from www.ncte.org/positions/statements/formative-assessment/formative-assessment_full.

Paul, R. & Elder, L. (2006). *The thinker's guide to the art of Socratic questioning*. Tomales, CA: The Foundation for Critical Thinking.

Popham, W. J. (2003). *Test better, teach better: The instructional role of assessment*. Alexandria, VA: Association for Supervision and Curriculum Development.

Popham, W. J. (2008). *Transformative assessment*. Alexandria, VA: Association for Supervision and Curriculum Development.

Popham, W. J. (2014). *Classroom assessment: What teachers need to know* (7th ed.). Upper Saddle River, NJ: Pearson Education.

Reeves, D. (2011). *Elements of grading: A guide to effective practice*. Bloomington, IN: Solution Tree.

Richards, R. (2015, March 10). *The qualitative formative assessment toolkit: Document learning with mobile technology*. Retrieved July 6, 2016 from Formative Assessment, www.edutopia.org/blog/qfat-document-learning-mobile-technology-reshan-richards.

Ridden, P., & Heldsinger, S. (2014). *What teachers need to know about assessment and reporting*. Camberwell, VA: ACER Press.

Ryshke, R. (2012, January 30). *When students "fail," should they be allowed do-overs?* Retrieved July 6, 2016 from https://rryshke.wordpress.com/2012/01/30/when-students-fail-should-they-be-allowed-do-overs/.

Sancisi, L., & Edgington, M. (2015). *Made to measure: Developing high quality observation, assessment, and planning in the early years*. Abingdon, UK: Routledge.

Schaaf, R. (2015). *Using digital games as assessment and instruction tools*. Bloomington, IN: Solution Tree Press.

Staff, T. (2016, January 10). 10 smart tools for digital exit slips. *TeachThought*. Retrieved July 6, 2016 from Uncategorized, www.teachthought.com/uncategorized/smart-tools-for-digital-exit-slips/.

Stanley, T. (2014). *Performance-based assessment for 21st-century skills: Provides real-world examples, breaks down the process into easy steps, contains ready-to-use reproducibles*. Waco, TX: Prufrock Press.

Stiggins, R. J. (2008). *An introduction to student-involved assessment for learning*. Upper Saddle River, NJ: Pearson.

Stiggins, R. J., & Conklin, N. F. (1992). *In teachers' hands: Investigating the practices of classroom assessment*. New York, NY: State University of New York Press.

Stockman, A. (2015, February 27). *Twenty creative ways to check for understanding—brilliant or insane* (Blog). Retrieved July 6, 2016 from Assessment, www.brilliant-insane.com/2015/02/twenty-creative-ways-check-understanding.html.

Stockman, A. (2015, June 17). *Beyond exit tickets: 11 fresh formative assessment strategies—brilliant or insane* (Blog). Retrieved July 6, 2016 from Assessment, www.brilliant-insane.com/2015/06/beyond-exit-tickets-11-fresh-formative-assessment-strategies.html.

Tomlinson, C., & Moon, T. (2013). *Assessment and student success in a differentiated classroom*. Alexandria, VA: Association for Supervision and Curriculum Development.

Vatterott, C. (2009). *Rethinking homework best practices that support diverse needs*. Alexandria, VA: Association for Supervision and Curriculum Development.

Waack, S. (2013). *Feedback in schools by John Hattie—Visible Learning* (Blog). Retrieved April 11, 2016 from http://visible-learning.org/2013/10/john-hattie-article-about-feedback-in-schools/.

Waack, S. (2016). *Glossary of Hattie's influences on student achievement—Visible Learning* (Blog). Retrieved July 6, 2016 from http://visible-learning.org/glossary/.

William, D., & Leahy, S. (2015). *Embedding formative assessment: Practical techniques for F-12 classrooms*. West Palm Beach, FL: Learning Sciences.

Wormeli, R. (2006). *Fair isn't always equal: Assessing and grading in the differentiated classroom*. Portland, ME: Stenhouse.

Taylor & Francis eBooks

Helping you to choose the right eBooks for your Library

Add Routledge titles to your library's digital collection today. Taylor and Francis ebooks contains over 50,000 titles in the Humanities, Social Sciences, Behavioural Sciences, Built Environment and Law.

Choose from a range of subject packages or create your own!

Benefits for you
>> Free MARC records
>> COUNTER-compliant usage statistics
>> Flexible purchase and pricing options
>> All titles DRM-free.

Benefits for your user
>> Off-site, anytime access via Athens or referring URL
>> Print or copy pages or chapters
>> Full content search
>> Bookmark, highlight and annotate text
>> Access to thousands of pages of quality research at the click of a button.

REQUEST YOUR FREE INSTITUTIONAL TRIAL TODAY

Free Trials Available
We offer free trials to qualifying academic, corporate and government customers.

eCollections – Choose from over 30 subject eCollections, including:

Archaeology	Language Learning
Architecture	Law
Asian Studies	Literature
Business & Management	Media & Communication
Classical Studies	Middle East Studies
Construction	Music
Creative & Media Arts	Philosophy
Criminology & Criminal Justice	Planning
Economics	Politics
Education	Psychology & Mental Health
Energy	Religion
Engineering	Security
English Language & Linguistics	Social Work
Environment & Sustainability	Sociology
Geography	Sport
Health Studies	Theatre & Performance
History	Tourism, Hospitality & Events

For more information, pricing enquiries or to order a free trial, please contact your local sales team:
www.tandfebooks.com/page/sales